RECOLLECTIONS
OF A FORMER SLAVE

CLASSICS IN BLACK STUDIES

RECOLLECTIONS OF A FORMER SLAVE

James L. Smith

WITH AN INTRODUCTION BY

Rosalyn Howard

Humanity Books

an imprint of Prometheus Books
59 John Glenn Drive, Amherst, New York 14228-2197

Cover image: From *Autobiography of James L. Smith*
(Norwich, CT: Press of the Bulletin Co., 1881).

Published by Humanity Books, an imprint of Prometheus Books

Inquiries should be addressed to
Humanity Books, 59 John Glenn Drive, Amherst, New York 14228–2197
VOICE: 716–691–0133, ext. 207; FAX: 716–564–2711
WWW.PROMETHEUSBOOKS.COM

08 07 06 05 04   5 4 3 2 1

Library of Congress Cataloging-in-Publication Data

Smith, James Lindsay.
    [Autobiography of James L. Smith]
    Recollections of a former slave / James L. Smith ; with an introduction
by Rosalyn Howard.
        p. cm. — (Classics in Black studies)
    Originally published: Autobiography of James L. Smith. Norwich
[Conn.] : Press of the Bulletin Co., 1881.
    ISBN 1–59102–204–5
    1. Smith, James Lindsay. 2. Slaves—Virginia—Biography. 3. Fugitive
slaves—United States—Biography. 4. Freedmen—United States—
Biography. 5. African Americans—Biography. 6. Slavery—Virginia—
Northern Neck—History—19th century. 7. Northern Neck (Va.)—
Biography. 8. Norwich (Conn.)—Biography. 9. African Americans—Social
conditions—19th century. I. Title. II. Series.

E444.S65 2004
306.3'62'092—dc22
[B]   2004042963

JAMES LINDSAY SMITH was born a slave on the plantation of Thomas Langsdon, in Northern Neck, Northumberland County, Virginia. One of eleven children of Rachel and Charles Payne, he was crippled at an early age with an injury that prevented him from working in the cotton fields. A house slave, he eventually was trained as a shoemaker and often hired out.

Smith's mother died after witnessing the sale of one of her children. His father died shortly after. Charles Payne's deathbed wish was that his children profess religion; this influenced Smith to become a preacher.

With two companions, Smith escaped in 1838, arriving first in Philadelphia, and then making his home with the family of a White pastor in Springfield, Massachusetts. Here he was employed in a shoe shop while attending school in nearby Wilbraham, Massachusetts. At this time, he was finally licensed to preach.

In 1842 Smith married Emeline Minerva Platt, with whom he had four children. He and his wife settled at Norwich, Connecticut, where Smith owned his own shop and purchased a home for his family. He continued his preaching at the Black Methodist church.

Smith published his *Autobiography of James L. Smith* in 1881. Besides telling his life story, he also wrote about the Black regiments in the Civil War and the conditions of African Americans after the war.

INTRODUCTION

Narratives of enslaved and formerly enslaved African Americans are some of the richest resources that provide a glimpse of the tragedies and triumphs of the African American experience of slavery. These narratives, especially those of the antebellum period, "form the bedrock tradition of African American literature."[1] The antebellum narratives served both literary and propaganda interests and were principally employed to expose the inhumanity of slavery and put an end to the "peculiar institution." As most enslaved persons were not permitted to become literate, indeed were under threat of death for attempting to do so, personal accounts are rare. From the millions of enslaved persons, only an estimated seventy of these narratives were recorded and published in the antebellum period. The most widely known was that of Frederick Douglass. Another fifty were published after the Civil War.[2]

These narratives are cultural artifacts, much like the material remains that archeologists unearth and use to interpret life in another age. They provide portraits, relative to individuals' life experiences, of existence during enslavement and after emancipation. James L. Smith's autobiography is among those published postbellum, a time when the audience for them was less receptive to the message. His rich narrative relates his life as a former slave, a shoemaker by trade, and an avocational preacher. He provides the reader with vivid details of severe beatings and other barbarous acts to which he and other slaves were subjected.

Smith's reasons for writing this autobiography were twofold. First, he believed that his was a fascinating account of transformation: life in bondage, escape to freedom, and successful (though still marginalized) assimilation into U.S. society. His portrait in the book's frontispiece shows a distinguished man who has successfully adopted the dress, and ostensibly mannerisms, of educated Whites. This portrait may also be interpreted as a vehicle for presenting to the public a nonthreatening image of an African American man, proffering an earnest account of his experiences.[3] Second, Smith sought to use the profits from the book to support himself in old age; as he states in his preface, the purchaser "will be assisting one who has been held in the chattels of slavery: who is now broken down with the infirmities of age, and asks your help to aid him in this, his means of support in his declining years."[4] Postbellum narratives, however, did not have the sizeable audiences that antebellum narratives enjoyed, which had made some of the latter highly profitable.

Smith believes that by publishing his own story, interspersed with rhetorical admonition, he can "ameliorate the condition of his now suffering people" and establish them as integral agents in the construction (with their free labor) and reconstruction of the nation. Smith also renders detailed accounts of various Civil War battles and identifies the valiant roles played by African Americans in their own liberation. He also reveals the diverse elements then extant in U.S. society; Smith experienced overt prejudice and discrimination, as well as kindness and support, on both sides of the Mason-Dixon line.

Smith published his narrative in 1881, sixteen years after the war's end, yet still a time of persistent discrimination against African Americans.[5] The legacy of slavery that has been the most difficult to eradicate is the hatred of people based upon their skin color. Indeed, even today this hatred continues to be "the most grievous wound to heal."[6] He chides those who devalue the intelligence of African Americans based upon a lack of literacy, a condition resulting directly from the circumstances of enslavement and not from any lack of intellectual capacity. Like Frederick Douglass, Smith views literacy and education as the essential elements on the path to freedom, self-respect, and opportunity for advancement. Lacking these elements, he said, "We must expect to be defrauded of our homes, our earnings, and our lands."

In addition to literacy and education, Smith views the Christian faith as central to this physical and psychological liberation. He admonishes White Christians who decry human rights abuses in foreign lands, yet who do not extend these same rights to African Americans at home, a theme familiar even today. Often employing Bible quotations to substantiate and illuminate his arguments, Smith suggests that the salvation of his people will become manifest only through the exercise of Christian duty. Occasionally an itinerant preacher, Smith speaks many times throughout the text as though from a pulpit, enumerating the evils that his people had suffered and continued to experience (often at the hands of professed Christians) and, at the same time, thanking his Christian God for sustaining them through these trials and tribulations.

Smith offers some insights into the causes of the Civil War and President Lincoln's motivations. He likens Lincoln to Moses delivering an enslaved people to the "Promised Land," while conversely acknowledging that freedom for African Americans was not Lincoln's primary goal. While he offers praise for Lincoln, he also counters with a pragmatic assessment of his actions.

Born into a family of twelve children, Smith initially lived in Northern Neck, Northumberland County, Virginia, on the plantation of Thomas Langsdon. It was there that he suffered an injury, one that fortuitously served to liberate him from the harsh labor traditionally performed by most enslaved persons on the plantation. He was crippled after a piece of heavy timber fell on his knee; the injury went untreated for a long time and resulted in a permanent impairment that made him useless in the cotton fields. Smith provides an illustration of crass inhumanity when he describes in detail his master's response when informed of the child's injury. Smith's mother took him to the "great house," related the incident, and implored the master to help them. Smith states that, "after hearing this sad news, he [the master] said he had niggers enough without me; I was not worth much anyhow, and he did not care if I did die." Smith was perceived only as chattel—property—and not very valuable property due to his young age. Now lame, he would be even less valuable. Had it not been for the "dressings" applied to his knee by the enslaved housekeeper in the "great house" he might have died.

Smith's lameness made him unfit for field work "so I had to do work about the house, to help the women. . . . I used to do chores about the house, and card rolls for the women." Smith relates the difficult life on the plantation, lack of food and proper clothing, and the barbaric beatings that many suffered for minor or suspected infractions. He gives another example of blatant inhumanity when his sister was sold to another plantation owner. Smith provides a poignant portrayal of his mother bearing this shock "in silent but bitter agony." He believes that this incident, heaped upon a mountain of other maltreatment, hastened her demise. His father died not long afterward, expressing a deathbed wish that his children should profess religion. This proved to be the impetus for Smith's career as a preacher: "From that day I commenced to seek the Lord with all my heart, and never stopped until I found Him." Smith's faith in God sustained him through the many trials of his life as an enslaved person, as a runaway, and as a freedman.

In chapter 1, "Birth and Childhood," Smith introduces us to his plantation birthplace in Virginia. He describes the crippling injury that enabled him to escape the rigors of the cotton fields. This chapter is filled with details about being moved from one plantation to another, the attempted poisoning of his father, his mother's death after witnessing the sale of one of her children, and his father's death not long thereafter. His own subsequent sale after becoming an orphan resulted in his being taught the trade of shoe making that would become his lifelong vocation.

Chapter 2, "Youth and Early Manhood," relates his cruel treatment at the hands of a shipmaster who took him from the plantation under the pretense of making him a sailor. What this new master essentially wanted was a slave on the sea rather than on land. Constantly beaten and starved, Smith attempted suicide by jumping ship, though soon after he had entered the water he thought better of it as he began to drown. After watching him flail helplessly for a while, the ship's captain pulled Smith from the water, only to beat him again.

Chapter 3, "Life in Heathsville," describes Smith's life at eighteen. He became so successful at his trade that he aroused the jealousy of his master. He also became a Christian and gained recognition as an eloquent speaker, often walking more than ten miles to prayer meetings, a feat especially remarkable because of his physical impairment. He describes these prayer meetings in elegant detail; they are reminiscent of Pentecostal church services with singing, hand clapping, and shouting pervading the congregation. Whites and the enslaved attended services in the same church building, but in different rooms. A strong Christian fervor gripped both congregations, leading to long meetings that occasionally lasted until dawn. Despite this Christian fraternity, slave catchers were permitted to enter and seize slaves in the midst of their hallelujahs. Smith also describes one of many acts of resistance that the enslaved employed; he secretly withheld a portion of his hired-out earnings in order to purchase a new suit, prompting someone to ask his master, "Who is master; Lindsey or you, for he dresses better than you do? Does he own you or do you own him?" It is in this chapter that we learn of his decision to escape.

Chapter 4, "Escape from Slavery," describes the challenges Smith faced in his pursuit of freedom. In comparison to other slaves, he led a relatively autonomous life. Working on a hired-out basis gave him an unusual amount of freedom of movement. Smith decided to cast his fate with a sailor he met who was also planning an escape. Joined by a third man, they began the fateful journey. It was during this escape that he saw a locomotive for the first time. The thundering sound of it frightened him: "I got sight of the fire and the smoke; said I 'it's the devil, it's the devil!'" He called the locomotive a "monster's head" and the cars attached to it "the wagons that he carries the souls to hell with." The fugitives ultimately arrived in Philadelphia and went their separate ways. Smith was aided by abolitionists and anti-slavery sympathizers on his journey to freedom, the final leg of which led him to the home of a White pastor in Springfield, Massachusetts.

In chapter 5, "Life in Freedom," Smith speaks of beginning "the first work I had ever done in the like of a freeman, which gave me the strength to think I was a man with others." The feeling of inferiority imposed by the yoke of slavery had prevented him from visualizing himself as a "real man." Smith took advantage of this new freedom to pursue an education. He "was very ambitious to learn, for I knew I would be better qualified to enter into business for myself. . . ." In Springfield he obtained a license to preach and befriended influential people who would further his career and efforts to spread the Gospel. However, this freedom in Springfield was not absolute. Life in the North still held many perils for Smith and others who had found sanctuary there. Slave catchers were tenacious and geography did not slow their pursuit; they had pro-slavery sympathizers in the North who informed upon runaways. The chapter ends with the announcement of Smith's marriage to Miss Emeline Minerva Platt in 1842.

In chapter 6, "Life in Norwich, Connecticut," Smith establishes a home and business to support himself and his new wife. All was not rosy for African Americans, free or enslaved, in Norwich. Discrimination was rampant there. Racists burned down his shop, and he was persecuted on every hand for succeeding in buying a house: "While many would be encouraged for their industry and toil, my people are subject to all sorts of abuse for buying desirable homes for their families." This attitude still exists more than a century later in some parts of the United States with racist practices such as redlining by bankers and real-estate brokers. Ironically, Smith states that "We were waiting with anxious expectation for the day to dawn, to enjoy all our privileges and equal rights as citizens." More than eighty years later, Martin Luther King Jr. was still "dreaming" for that same day to dawn.

In chapter 7, "The War of the Rebellion," Smith reflects on the Civil War, remarking that President Lincoln's Emancipation Proclamation was not issued because of any desire to end the enslavement of African peoples. Instead, Smith states, "Our martyred president, proud in the strength of his high position said, 'the Union must be saved with slavery, if it can, without it, if it must.'" Lincoln's primary goal was to save the Union at all costs. Smith perceives the hand of the Almighty in this war: "to the observing eye, the hand of God has been seen in the . . . overthrow of the proud, and uplifting of the lowly; seen in the fall of the taskmaster and the emancipation of the slave. Many fought for the liberation of the colored man, although they hated him."

Initially, some "Yankees" had expressed anger at the thought of serving alongside Black troops, and Smith quotes one as stating, "I will never die by the side of a nigger." Northern resistance to Black troops bearing arms in defense of the Union finally subsided in the face of the desperate need for more troops. Many Northerners also realized how valuable former slaves could be to the war effort. These Blacks knew the terrain and the habits of Southern slaveholders. The Union acquiesced and admitted them as "laborers" in name, but fighting troops in actuality. Regiments of African Americans fought valiantly, receiving little or no wages, and dispelled the myths that many Whites had about their willingness to fight.

In the beginning of chapter 8, "After the War," Smith

recalls the precarious nature of freedom for African Americans in the antebellum period, as the Fugitive Slave Law imposed strict penalties. He describes his commitment to resist reenslavement at all costs: "I had determined never to be taken back alive. Death was preferable to slavery, now that I had tasted the sweets of liberty." Although his "sweet liberty" held many challenges, it was far better than what he had experienced in the past. After Emancipation he makes a triumphal return to his former home in Heathsville, which he had escaped from thirty years before. His reunion with family members and friends, setting foot on his old homeland, was bittersweet indeed. Ironically, he was invited to have dinner with his former mistress in the "great house." Smith describes with glee how the fortunes of former "negro traders" had changed; they were now the ones in tattered clothes, begging for meals from the freedmen.

Chapter 9 is entitled "Conclusion," but it does not actually end the book, for three more chapters follow. In it Smith relates the celebration in Norwich of the passage of the Fifteenth Amendment to the United States Constitution in 1870. The Fifteenth Amendment guaranteed the right to vote, a right that "shall not be denied or abridged by the United States or by any State on account of race, color, or previous condition of servitude." Even this legislation did not, as Smith states, end the challenges for the newly freed peoples: "We are just crossing the bitter waters, and can scarcely see our landing; we are not safe over, yet we hope to escape the storms that are still beating upon us, and moor our bark on the shore of freedom. . . . My whole race is yet in peril, and God only knows the end."

In chapter 10, "Colored Men During the War," Smith laments the obscuration of the heroism of "colored troops" by historians in the United States. He quotes at length a letter describing the aid that enslaved persons provided to Union soldiers. The Confederates, in an attempt to maintain the loyalty of their slaves, offered them freedom for joining the Confederate cause. Of course, the enslaved realized that this was not to their benefit. Although some appeared to go along with this deal, it was a ruse; they waited for the opportune time to seek their freedom. Smith proudly describes the heroic deeds of the African American regiments from Kansas, Connecticut, North Carolina, and Massachusetts.

Smith shows how racism persisted after Emancipation in chapter 11, "Recollections of the War." Some states refused to recognize the end of the war and, with that, the end of slavery and persecution of African Americans. Free persons of color, being subjected to harsh penalties for not observing curfews, sent a delegation to Washington, DC, where they received assurances of protection from the president. Smith reiterates here various battles and the bravery of African American troops during the war.

In the final chapter, "The Exodus," Smith portrays the bittersweet harvest of Emancipation. Many freedmen suffered under inhumane conditions, no longer having the means to make a living or to obtain food, clothing, or shelter. Some former slaveholders conscripted freedmen to work on the same plantations for extremely low wages. Freedmen were also harassed by "night raiders." Many migrated to Washington seeking federal assistance. But government aid was not sufficient to meet the needs of the great number of these destitute freedmen. Many died of exposure or starvation there, Smith says, especially the children. Various aid organizations were employed to help relieve their misery. Other freedmen migrated west where they faced new challenges among another decimated and dispersed people, the Native Americans.

Smith's narrative, written during a time of monumental societal change in the United States, illuminates the complexity of human nature and relationships. It invites us to probe history through a firsthand account of the experiences of a man who did not achieve fame, but whose remarkable life likely mirrored those of many voiceless former slaves who achieved freedom through great sacrifice, courage, and determination. His invaluable story deserves a place among the canon of "classic" slave narratives. The republication of Smith's autobiography significantly recaptures an important piece of history and allows us an appreciation for the resilience of the human spirit in the pursuit of freedom.

Rosalyn Howard, PhD
Assistant Professor of Anthropology
University of Central Florida

Notes

1. William L. Andrews Jr., *The Civitas Anthology of African American Slave Narratives* (Washington, DC: Civitas/Counterpoint, 1999), p. 1.
2. Ibid.
3. See Folsom for a similar discussion about the portrait of Frederick Douglass on the frontispiece of his *Narrative.* Ed Folsom, "Portrait of the Artist as a Young Slave: Douglass's Frontispiece Engravings," in *Approaches to Teaching Narrative of the Life of Frederick Douglass,* ed. James C. Hall (New York: Modern Language Association of America, 1999), pp. 55–65.
4. James L. Smith, *Autobiography of James L. Smith* (Norwich, CT: Press of the Bulletin Company, 1881), p. ix.

5. Also published in the year 1881 was Frederick Douglass's postbellum memoir, *The Life and Times of Frederick Douglass.*

6. John Hope Franklin, *From Slavery to Freedom: A History of Negro Americans* (1947; reprint, New York: Alfred A. Knopf, 1967).

RECOLLECTIONS
OF A FORMER SLAVE

James L. Smith

TO THE MEMORY OF
MY FATHER,

CHARLES PAYNE,

WHO LIES IN A NAMELESS,
UNKNOWN GRAVE,
THIS VOLUME
IS DEDICATED.

PREFACE

The writer would bring before the public the narrative of his life while in bondage, which is substantially true in all its details. The painful wrongs inflicted then and now have caused the writer, though many years have passed, to take up the publication of this narrative of himself. There are many incidents and characters described in this narrative personally known to the writer, which make him anxious to put forth some effort, however humble it may be, to ameliorate the condition of his now suffering people, in order that the facts may confirm the truthful saying: "My people will be styled a nation yet, and also claim their nationality." For this they have fought and suffered hundreds of years in servitude and bondage. It is a fact which ought to thrill the heart of every American citizen to see the interest they take in learning; the untiring exertions they make to overcome every obstacle, even death itself to acquire it. It is what God has promised: "To be a God to the faithful and to their seed after them."

The writer hopes not to weary your patience in reviewing his narrative, which is fraught with so many exciting scenes. It is the duty of men to occupy places of power and trust, therefore our rulers, above all others, ought to be holy and devoted men. There are, however, some found in every age of the world who believe in freedom of thought and speech; and many who are untiring in their efforts to secure the future well-being of those intrusted to their care; it affords the most powerful argument to influence the minds of some. It is believed that no one who reads attentively, and reflects seriously, will doubt that the time is near at hand, which is spoken of by God: "Ye shall let my people go free." Now the great revolution seems to me to have come; now is the time for us to act in trying to save that which was lost; in stimulating them to education; and in building homes and schoolhouses for their children, that they may become honorable and respectable citizens of the States to which they have acceded. We want earnest laborers amongst us, for those who are instructing my people are few and far between; and we have been deprived of education by the hand of slavery and servitude, which has been brought upon us by the slave-holder. I feel it is the duty of the people to take up our cause, and instruct wherever they can.

Our ignorance, which is often spoken of, and for which we are not to blame, is caused by this ill, slavery; and the whipping post was resorted to if any attempt was made to learn the alphabet. I can say in the fullness of my heart that there is no darkness equal to this, not even the Egyptian darkness which is spoken of by missionaries now laboring in foreign lands. I only pray to hope on, and on, that God may appear in our behalf, and let the sun of civilization and education be extended among my people until it shall reach from sea to sea, and from land to land. Then shall Ethiopia stretch forth her hand unto God and call you blessed. I thank God for what I have seen and experienced so far in regard to the amelioration of our condition as a people. I hardly expect to see the completion of the act of liberty which was commenced by our most earnest friend, Senator Sumner. "See to the Civil Rights Bill; don't let it fail," were among his last words to his associate who stood beside the dying senator.

This volume speaks of our earnest desire for more liberty and rights as a free people, and that our children may enjoy that of which we have been deprived. Never was the effectiveness of our Christian instrumentalities in other lands more dependent than now upon the vigorous and progressive development of Christian principles at home.

As we are entering upon a new decade our thoughts go back to 1861; and what a period is this to review! Could we have held the glass to our vision and seen what the nation would accomplish in its terrible struggle for existence, who would not have shrunk from the almost miraculous undertaking? But God had the blank years before Him, and as they passed, He proceeded to fill out the record. Nineteen years ago we were rocking in the swell of the gathering storm which was so soon and unexpectedly to break in its fury, and who could tell how many were to perish and go down ere its fury should be spent. In the strike which slavery made for the ascendancy, how little did we know through what terrible revulsions it would pass on its way to destruction. The cry was, "slavery must go down." How many mighty obstacles must fall before the march of the avalanche. How many disputed the question at the time, as to how this should be accomplished. But like the great iceberg when soft winds blow, and gentle rays fall on it, whether God would prostrate it as he does great cities when earthquakes rock them, was the question to be considered. Such was our uncertainty then; but these counsels were made known to us more speedily than we dreamed.

We have seen how how the system of slavery was to be destroyed; and there is work for the Christian Church, there are responsibilities on Christian hearts which we did not anticipate nineteen years ago. National politics have brought about many incidental questions; but there is a period of new and aggressive work in which we are led to go forward and possess the land. Such a burden of duty as it bears upon us at this time, to remember that we are hourly approaching opportunities and responsibilities greater than we have hitherto known. In this spirit we have labored for the grand conquests which to-day are calling us onward. In this spirit we must toil now. How much we ask, bringing to you our pressing wants—come over and help us, for my people are in need of instruction, both spiritual and educational; and in thus aiding us you will accomplish a work of far reaching power, of which you have now no comprehension. "If God be for us, who can be against us?"

May this narrative awaken some to still greater earnestness in working for Christ, and freedom through the land. "Be not weary in well doing, for in due season ye shall reap if ye faint not." It is my privilege to speak about the impoverished people of the South, and those main pillars of our Republic, the Church and the School: thus following up the victories of our arms with the sublimer victories of Christian love. What tremendous agencies God has employed within these few years, and what He has caused to be exerted for all generations to come; and if there is one scripture which is most forcibly illustrated and impressed upon me than any other, it is this: "Whereas ye know not what shall be on the morrow." Who could have foreseen how much God would bring to pass in these nineteen years? Could the author have held the glass to his vision, and seen what the nation would accomplish in its terrible struggle for existence, he would have despaired; but as the period has arrived, my people are determined to go forward and possess the land which will bring our children within the pale of intellectual training in the institutions of education and religion; for we all know that without this education we must expect to be defrauded of our homes, our earnings, and our lands. Many only make their mark in signing their names, for they cannot read or write.

This is the secret of their not having any thing to-day and the responsibility rests on you, Christian people of these United States of America; and the cry is for help now. There is not a nation under heaven that needs more sympathy and pity from the people of the United States than my people; for they are maltreated every way in the higher educational schools, while endeavoring to obtain an education.

During the most eventful period in our history, the little stream of light that began to flow in Virginia and the Mississippi Valley has from year to year widened and deepened, and rolled with mighty healing power. It has passed the dividing mountains, and carried a flood of Divine blessings to many of my people. "But blessed are your eyes, for they see, and your ears, for they hear: for verily I say unto you, that many prophets and righteous men have desired to see these things which ye see, and have not seen them, and to hear these things which ye hear, and have not heard them." We still have hope of saving our beloved people, and of seeing prosperity in the future. Many of the colored people deserve much of this country for what they did and suffered in the great national struggle. When the Rebels appeared in their strength, and defeat followed defeat in quick succession, while the government was bleeding at every pore, and there appeared to be no help or power to save the Union, then our colored soldiers came to its timely aid and fought like brave men. The rebel lion struck at the very heart of our country. Many of them were ill-treated by the Union soldiers—many a colored soldier was knocked down by them, and maltreated in every way. The treatment the colored soldiers received from the hands of the white soldiers was equal to slavery. All this was because the white soldiers did not want to stand side by side with them—did not want the negro in the ranks. Pen can not begin to describe the extreme sufferings of the colored men in this respect. The Yankee soldiers were eager for glory; the idea of having a colored man in the ranks caused many of them to be angry. "I will never die by the side of a nigger," was uttered from the lips of many.

I hope this work may find its way into the homes and hearts of those who are endeavoring still to help us in our efforts for liberty; if I succeed in this, it is all I desire. That I may have the prayers of all who are interested in my behalf, is the earnest desire of the writer.

In purchasing this narrative you will be assisting one who has been held in the chattels of slavery: who is now broken down by the infirmities of age, and asks your help to aid him in his, his means of support in his declining years.

CONTENTS

Chapter I: Birth and Childhood   35

Birthplace—Parentage—Accident from disobedience—
Sickness—Crippled for life—Death of master and change
of situation—Cecilia—Jealousy, and attempt to take the life
of my father by poisoning—Discovery and punishment—
Removal to Northern Neck—Mode of living in old Virginia—Experiences of slave life—A cruel mistress—Work
on plantation—Feigning sickness—Death of father and
mother—Bound out to a trade—A brutal master.

Chapter II: Youth and Early Manhood   49

Cook on board a ship—A heartless master—An unsavory
breakfast, and punishment—A difficult voyage—Tired of
life, and attempt at suicide—Escape—Life on plantation—
A successful ruse—Removal to Heathsville.

Chapter III: Life in Heathsville 57

Hired out—Religious experience, conversion—Work as
an exhorter—A slave prayer meeting—Over worked—
A ludicrous accident—Love of dress—Love of freedom—
Death of my master—Religious exercises forbidden—
A stealthy meeting—The surprise—Fairfield Church—
Quarterly meeting—Nancy Merrill—A religious meeting
and a deliverance—Sleeping at my post.

Chapter IV: Escape from Slavery 67

Change of master—Plans of escape—Fortune telling—
Zip—A lucky nap—Farewell—Beginning of the escape—
A prosperous sail—Arrival at Frenchtown—Continuing on
foot—Exhausted—Deserted by companions—Hesitating—
Terrible fright—A bold resolve and a hearty breakfast—
Re-union at New Castle—Passage to Philadelphia—A
final farewell—Trouble and anxiety—A friend—Passage to
New York, Hartford and Springfield—A warm welcome—
Dr. Osgood.

Chapter V: Life in Freedom 87

Employment in a shoe shop—Education at Wilbraham—
Licensed to preach—John M. Brown—Mrs. Cecelia
Platt—Elizabeth Osgood—Sabbath and Mission Schools—
Return to Springfield—Engagement with Dr. Hudson—
Experience at Saybrook—Persecutions of Abolitionists—
Lecturing—Courtship and marriage.

Chapter VI: Life in Norwich, Conn.   99

Came to Norwich—Started business—Purchase a house—
Persecutions and difficulties—Ministerial labors—Church
troubles—Formation of a new Methodist Church—
Retiring from ministerial work—Amos B. Herring—Mary
Humphreys—Sketches of life and customs in Africa.

Chapter VII: The War of the Rebellion   107

Desire to return to Virginia—Opening of the War—
Disdain of the aid of colored men—Defeat—Progress of
the War—Employing colored men—Emancipation Procla-
mation—Celebration—Patriotism of Colored Soldiers—
Bravery at Port Hudson—Close of the War—Death of
Lincoln—A tribute to Senator Sumner—Passage of the
Civil Rights Bill—Our Standard Bearers.

Chapter VIII: After the War   119

Fear of capture—A visit to Heathsville—Father Christmas,
and a children's festival—Preaching at Washington—My
first visit to my old home—Joy and rejoicing—Meeting
my old mistress—My old cabin home—The old spring—
Change of situations—The old doctor—Improvement in
the condition of the colored people—Buying homes—
Industry.

Chapter IX: Conclusion 135

The Fifteenth Amendment Celebration—The parade—
Address—Collation—Charles L. Remond—Closing words.

Chapter X: Colored Men During the War 141

In battle—Kindness to Union men—Devotion to the
Union—29th Conn.—Its departure—Return—The noble
Kansas troops—54th Mass.—Obedient to orders.

Chapter XI: Recollections of the War 155

The spirit of the South—Delaware—Kentucky—
Meetings—Conventions—Gen. Wild's raid—Slave
heroism—A reminiscence of 1863—Sherman's march
through Georgia—Arming the slave.

Chapter XII: The Exodus 169

Arrival of negroes in Washington—Hospitality of
Washington people—Suffering and privation—Education
of the freedmen—Causes of emigration—Cruelty at the
South—Prejudice at the North—Hopes for the future.

LIST OF
ILLUSTRATIONS

I | BIRTH AND CHILDHOOD

Birthplace—Parentage—Accident from disobedience—
Sickness—Crippled for life—Death of master and change
of situation—Cecilia—Jealousy, and attempt to take the
life of my father by poisoning—Discovery and
punishment—Removal to Northern Neck—Mode of
living in old Virginia—Experiences of slave life—
A cruel mistress—Work on plantation—Feigning
sickness—Death of father and mother—Bound out to a
trade—A brutal master.

My birthplace was in Northern Neck, Northumberland County, Virginia. My mother's name was Rachel, and my father's was Charles. Our cabin home was just across the creek. This creek formed the head of the Wycomco River. Thomas Langsdon, my master, lived on one side of the creek, and my mother's family—which was very large—on the opposite side. Every year a new comer was added to our humble cabin home, till she gave birth to the eleventh child. My mother had just so much cotton to spin every day as her stint. I lived here till I was quite a lad.

There was a man who lived near us whose name was

Haney, a coach maker by trade. He always had his timber brought up to the creek. One day he ordered one of his slave women to go down and bring up some of the timber. She took with her a small lad, about my size, to assist her. She came along by our cabin, as it was near the place where the timber was, and asked me to go along with her to help her. I asked mother if I could go. She decidedly said "No!" As my mother was sick, and confined to her bed at that time, I took this opportunity to steal away, unknown to her. We endeavored, at first, to carry a large piece of timber—the woman holding one end, I the other, and the boy in the middle. Before we had gone far her foot struck something that caused her to fall, so that it jarred my end, causing it to drop on my knee. The boy being in the middle, the full weight of the timber fell on his foot, crushing and mangling it in a most shocking manner. After this accident, the woman and boy started for home, carrying some smaller pieces of timber with them.

After a few days of painful sickness, mortification took place in the little boy's foot, and death claimed him for his own. My grandmother hearing my voice of distress came after me and brought me home. At the time she did not think I was hurt very seriously. My mother called me to her bedside and punished me for disobeying her. After a day or two my knee began to contract, to shrink. This caused my mother to feel that there was something very serious about it, and as soon as she was able to get around, she went to the "great house," the home of Thos. Langsdon, and told him that I was badly hurt, and that something must be done for me. He asked her what was the matter. She told him what had happened to me, and how seriously I was hurt with the timber. After hearing this sad news, he said he had niggers enough without me; I was not worth much any how, and he did not care if I did die. He positively declared that he should not employ a physician for me. As there was no medical remedy applied to my knee, it grew worse and worse until I could not touch my foot to the ground without the most intense pain. There was a doctor in the neighborhood at this time, and mother knowing it sent me to see him, unknowingly to my master. He examined my knee and said, as it had been out of joint so long it would be a difficult matter to break it over again and then set it. He told my mother to take me home and bathe it in cold spring water to prevent it from ulcerating, for if it should it would kill me.

When I was able to walk around with my lameness, Thomas Langsdon took me across the creek to his house to do chores. I was then quite a boy. After a while my leg commenced swelling, and after that ulcerating. It broke in seven places. I was flat on my back for seven or eight weeks before I could raise myself without help. I suffered every thing but death itself, and would have died if it had not been for Miss Ayers, who was house-keeper in the "great house." She came into the kitchen every day to dress my knee, till I could get around. Not having any shoes, and being exposed to the weather, I took a heavy cold which caused my knee to ulcerate. When I was able to get around, the father of my young master was taken sick, and was confined to his bed for months. I, with another boy about my size and age—six or seven years—sat by his bedside. We took our turns alternately, the boy so many hours and I so many, to keep the flies off from him. After a while the old man died, then I was relieved from fighting or contending with flies.

After this I went across the creek to help my mother, as I was not large enough to be of any service on the plantation. In the course of time my young master died, also his wife, leaving two sons, Thomas and John Langsdon. My young master chose for us (slaves) a guardian, who hired us all out. As my mother gave birth to so many children, it made her not very profitable as a servant, and instead of being let out to the highest bidder, was let out to the lowest one that would support her for the least money. Hence my father, though a slave, agreed to take her and the children, and support them for so much money.

My father's master had a brother by the name of Thad. Guttridge, who lived in Lancaster County, who died, leaving his plantation to his brother, (my father's master). My father was then sent to take charge of this new plantation, and moved my mother and the children with him into the "great house;" my mother as mistress of the house.

This Thad. Guttridge had a woman by the name of Cecilia, or Cella, as she was called, whom he kept as house-keeper and mistress, by whom he had one child, a beautiful girl almost white. After this new arrangement was made for my father to take charge of the new plantation, this woman Cella, was turned out of her position as house-keeper to a field hand, to work on the plantation in exchange with my mother.

This was not very agreeable to Cella, so she sought or contrived some plan to avenge herself. So one Saturday night Cella went off, and did not return till Sunday night. When she did return she brought with her some whisky, in two bottles. She asked father if he would like to take a dram; and, not thinking there would be any trouble resulting from it, he replied: "Yes." Giving him the bottle, he took a drink. She then gave the other bottle to my mother, and she took a drink. Afterwards, Cella gave us children some out of the same bottle that my mother drank from. Father went to bed that night, complaining of not feeling very well. The next morning he was worse, and continued to grow worse until he was very low. His master was immediately sent for, who came in great haste. On his arrival he found father very low, not able to speak aloud. My master, seeing in what a critical condition he was, sent for a white doctor, who came, and gave father some medicine. He grew worse every time he took the medicine. There was an old colored doctor who lived some ten miles off. Some one told Bill Guttridge that he had better see him, and, perhaps he could tell what was the matter with my father. Bill Guttridge went to see this colored doctor.

The doctor looked at his cards, and told him that his Charles was poisoned, and even told him who did it, and her motive for doing it. Her intention was to get father and mother out of their place, so that she could get back again. Little did she think that the course she took would prove a failure. The doctor gave Guttridge a bottle of medicine, and told him to return in haste, and give father a dose of it. He did so. I saw him coming down the lane towards the house, at full speed. He jumped off his horse, took his saddle-bags and ran into the house. He called my mother to give him a cup, so he could pour out some of the medicine. He then raised my father up, and gave him some of it out of the cup. After he had laid him down, and replaced the covering over him again, he took his hickory cane and went out into the kitchen—Cella sat here with her work—with an oath told her: "You have poisoned my Charles." He had no sooner uttered these words, when he flew at her with his cane. As he was very much enraged, he commenced beating her over the head and shoulders till he had worn the cane out. After he had stopped beating her in this brutal manner her head was swollen or puffed to such size that it was impossible to recognize who she was; she did not look like the same woman. Not being satisfied with this punishment, he told her that he intended repeating it in the morning. In the morning, when he went to look for her, she was gone. He stayed with father till he was able to sit up. When he returned home—which was about ten miles—he left word with father that if Cella came home, to bind her and send her down to him.

This was in the fall of the year. Some months passed before we saw Cella again. The following spring, while the men were cleaning up the new land, Cella came to them; they took and brought her to the house. Father was then able to walk about the house, but was unable to work much. He had her tied, and put behind a man on horseback and carried down to his master, who took her and put her on board a vessel to be sent to Norfolk. He sold her to some one there. This was the last time we ever saw, or heard from her.

We lived here quite a number of years on Lancaster plantation. Finally my father's master sold it, and also his brother's daughter, Cella's child. We then returned from Lancaster plantation to Northern Neck, Va., and lived nearly in the same place, called Hog Point; we lived here quite a number of years. Mr. Dick Mitchell, my master's guardian, took me away from my mother to Lancaster County, on his plantation, where I lived about six months. I used to do chores about the house, and card rolls for the women. Being lame unfitted me for a field hand, so I had to do work about the house, to help the women.

Our dress was made of tow cloth; for the children, nothing was furnished them but a shirt; for the older ones, a pair of pantaloons or a gown, in addition, according to the sex. Besides these, in the winter season an overcoat, or a round jacket; a wool hat once in two or three years for the men, and a pair of coarse brogan shoes once a year. We dwelt in log cabins, and on the bare ground. Wooden floors were an unknown luxury to the slave. There were neither furniture nor bedsteads of any description; our beds were collections of straw and old rags, thrown down in the corners; some were boxed in with boards, while others were old ticks filled with straw. All ideas of decency and refinement were, of course, out of the question.

Our mode of living in Virginia was not unlike all other slave states. At night, each slept rolled up in a coarse blanket; one partition, which was an old quilt or blanket, or something else that answered the purpose, was extended across the hut; wood partitions were unknown to the doomed slave. A water pail, a boiling pot, and a few gourds made up the furniture. When the corn had been ground in a hand-mill, and then boiled, the pot was swung from the fire and the children squatted around it, with oyster shells for spoons. Sweet potatoes, oysters and crabs varied the diet. Early in the morning the mothers went off to the fields in companies, while some women too old to do anything but wield a stick were left in charge of the strangely silent and quiet babies. The field hands having no time to prepare any thing for their morning meals, took up hastily a piece of hoe-cake and bacon, or any thing that was near at hand, and then, with rakes or hoes in the hand, hurried off to the fields at early dawn, for the loud horn called them to their labors. Heavy were their hearts as they daily traversed the long cotton rows. The overseer's whip took no note of aching hearts.

The allowance for the slave men for the week was a peck-and-a-half of corn meal, and two pounds of bacon. The women's allowance was a peck of meal, and from one pound-and-a-half to two pounds of bacon; and so much for each child, varying from one-half to a peck a week, and of bacon, from one-half to a pound a week. In order to make our allowance hold out, we went crabbing or fishing. In the winter season we used to go hunting nights, catching oysters, coons and possums. When I was home, the slaves used to bake their hoe-cakes on hoes; these hoes were larger than those used in the northern states. Another way for cooking them was to rake the ashes and then put the meal cake between the ashes and the fire—this was called ash pone; and still another way was to bake the bare cake in a Dutch oven, heated for the purpose—that was called oven pone. This latter way of baking them was much practiced, or customary at the home of the slave-holders.

The "great house," so called by the plantation hands, was the home where the master and his family lived. The kitchen was an apartment by itself in the yard, a little distance from the "great house," so as to face the front part of the house; others were built in the back yard. The kitchens had one bed-room attached to them.

One night I went crabbing, and was up most all night; a boy accompanied me. We caught a large mess of crabs, and took them home with us. The next day I had to card for one of the women to spin, and, being up all night, I could hardly keep my eyes open; every once in a while I would fall asleep. Mrs. Mitchell could look through her window into the kitchen, it being in front of the "great house." She placed herself in the portico, to see that I worked. When I fell into a quiet slumber she would halloo out and threaten to cowhide me; but, for all that, I could not keep awake. Seeing that I did not heed her threatenings, she took her rawhide and sewing and seated herself close by me, saying she would see if she could keep me awake. She asked me what was the matter; I told her I felt sick. (I was a great hand to feign sickness). She asked me what kind of sickness; I told her I had the stomach ache and could not work. Thinking that something did ail me, she sent Alfred, the slave boy, into the house after her medicine chest; she also told him to bring her the decanter of whisky. She then poured out a tumbler most full of whisky and then made me drink all of it. After drinking it I was worse than I was before, for I was so drunk I could not see what I was doing. Every once in a while when I fell asleep she would give me a cut with the rawhide. At last, night came and I was relieved from working so steady. When I was not carding I was obliged to knit; I disliked it very much; I was very slow; it used to take me two or three weeks to knit one stocking, and when I had finished it you could not tell what the color was.

I had also to drive the calves for the milk-woman to milk. One afternoon, towards night, I stopped my other work to hunt up the calves and have them at the cow-pen by the time the milk-woman came, with the cows; I went in one of the quarters, and being tired, I sat down on a bench, and before I knew it I fell asleep and slept until after dark. The milk-woman came with the cows, but there were no calves there. She hallooed for me, but I was not within hearing. As the cow-pen was not far from the "great house" the mistress heard her. At last the milk-woman came to the "great house" to see what had become of me, but no Lindsey could be found. She went to the kitchen where the milk pails were kept, took them, and then drove the calves up herself and went to milking. Before she had finished, I awoke and started for the kitchen for the pails. When I got there, Mrs. Mitchell was standing up in the middle of the kitchen floor. She asked me where I had been; I told her I fell asleep in the quarters' and forgot myself. She said she would learn me how to attend to my business, so she told Alfred to go into the "great house" and bring her the rawhide. I stood there trembling about mid-way of the floor. Taking the cow-hide, and lifting her large arms as high as she could, applied it to my back. The sharp twang of the rawhide, as it struck my shoulders, raised me from the floor.

Jinny (the cook) told me afterwards, that when Mrs. Mitchell struck me I jumped about four feet, and did not touch the floor again till I was out doors. She followed me to the door and just had time to see me turn the corner of the "great house." I then ran down towards the cow-pen. The cook told me the way I was running as I turned the corner, that she did not believe that there was a dog or horse on the plantation that could have caught me. I went to the cow-pen and helped the woman to finish milking, and stayed around till I thought that Mrs. Mitchell had gone into the "great house." But to my astonishment when I went to the kitchen again, behold, there she was still waiting for me. She asked me why I ran from her; I told her that it hurt me so bad when she struck me, that I did not know that I was running. She said the next time she whipped me that she would have me tied, then she guessed I would not run. She let me off that night by promising her that I would do better, and never run from her again.

Mrs. Mitchell was a very cruel woman; I have seen her whip Jinny in a very brutal manner. There was a large shade tree that stood in the yard; she would make Jinny come out under this tree, and strip her shoulders all bare; then she would apply the rawhide to her bare back until she had exhausted her own strength, and was obliged to call some of the house servants to bring her a chair. While she was resting, she would keep Jinny still standing. After resting her weary arms, she commenced again. Thus she whipped and rested, till she had applied fifty blows upon her suffering back. There was not a spot upon her naked back to lay a finger but there would be a gash, gushing forth the blood; every cut of the rawhide forced an extraordinary groan from the suffering victim; she then sent her back to the kitchen, with her back sore and bleeding, to her work. We slaves often talked the matter over amongst ourselves, and wondered why God suffered such a cruel woman to live. One night, as we were talking the matter over, Jinny exclaimed: "De Lord bless me, chile, I do not believe dat dat devil will ever die, but live to torment us."

After a while I left there for Hog Point, to live with my mother. In the course of a year or two old Mrs. Mitchell sickened, and died.

After she died, I went down to see the folks on the plantation. After my arrival, they told me that just before she breathed her last, she sent for Jinny to come to her bedroom. As she entered, she looked up and said: "Jinny, I am going to die, and I suppose you are glad of it." Jinny replied: "No, I am not." After pretending to cry, she came back to the kitchen and exclaimed: "Dat old devil is going to die, and I am glad of it." When her mistress died her poor back had a brief respite for a while. I do not know what took place upon the plantation after this.

As my young master became of age about this time, Mr. Mitchell gave the guardianship to him. During this time my mother died; then I was bound out to his uncle, John Langsdon, to learn the shoe-maker's trade. John Langsdon was a very kind man, and struck me but once the whole time I was with him in Fairfield, and then it was my own fault. One day, while I was at work in the shop, I put my work down and went out; while I was out, I stepped into the "great house." His two sons were in the house shelling corn; some words passed between his eldest son and me, which resulted in a fight. Mr. Langsdon was looking out of the shop window and saw us fighting; so he caught up a stick and struck me three or four times, and then drove me off to the shop to my work. I took hold of shoe-making very readily; I had not been there a great while when I could make a shoe, or a boot—this I acquired by untiring industry. He used to give me my stint, a pair of shoes a day. I remained with him four years.

The first cruel act of my master, as soon as he became of age, and took his slaves home, was to sell one of my mother's children, whose name was Cella, who was carried off by a trader. We never saw or heard from her again. Oh! how it rent my mother's heart; although her heart was almost broken by grief and despair, she bore this shock in silent but bitter agony. Her countenance exhibited an anxious and sorrowful expression, and her manner gave evidence of a deep settled melancholy. This, and other troubles which she was compelled to pass through, and constant toil and exposure so shattered her physical frame that disease soon preyed upon her, that hastened her to the grave. Ah! I saw not the death-angel, as with white wings he approached. When the hour came for her departure from earth there was but a slight struggle, a faint gasp, and the freed spirit went to its final home. Gone where there are neither bonds nor tortures, sorrow and weeping are unknown.

My mother was buried in a field where there was no other dead deposited; no stone marks her resting place; no fragrant flowers adorn the sod that covers her silent house.

My father soon followed my mother to the grave; then we children were left fatherless and motherless in the cold world. My father's death was very much felt as a good servant, being quick and energetic, rendered him a favorite with his master. When my father was about to die, he called his children, those who were at home around him, as no medicine could now retard the steady approach of the death-angel. When we assembled about him he bade us all farewell, saying, there was but one thing that troubled him, and that was, not one of us professed religion. When I heard that, and saw his sunken eye and hollow cheek, my heart sank within me. Oh! how those words did cut me, like a two-edged sword. From that day I commenced to seek the Lord with all my heart, and never stopped till I found Him. After my father's death, my eldest sister took charge of the younger children, until her master took her home.

One cold morning, while I lived at Hog Point, we looked out and saw three men coming towards the house. One was Mr. Haney, the other one was one of his neighbors, and the last one was his slave. Near our cabin home was a large oak tree; they took this doomed slave down to this tree, and stripped him entirely naked; then they threw a rope across a limb and tied him by his wrists, and drew him up so that his feet cleared the ground. They then applied the lash to his bare back till the blood streamed and reddened the ground underneath where he hung. After whipping him to their satisfaction, they took him down, and led him bound through our yard. I looked at him as he passed, and saw the great ridges in his back as the blood was pouring out of them, and it was as a dagger to my heart. They took him and forced him to work, with his back sore and bleeding. He came to our cabin, a night or two afterwards; my mother asked him what Mr. Haney beat him for; he said it was for nothing only because he did not work enough for him; he did all he could, but the unreasonable master demanded more. I never saw him any more, for shortly after this we moved away.

YOUTH AND
EARLY MANHOOD

Cook on board a ship—A heartless master—
An unsavory breakfast, and punishment—A difficult
voyage—Tired of life, and attempt at suicide—Escape—
Life on plantation—A successful ruse—Removal to
Heathsville.

W hen I lived at Mrs. Mitchell's there was a man
who owned a vessel, who came there and took
our grain. He told Mr. Mitchell he would like to take me
and make a sailor of me. He liked the looks of my countenance very much, so they struck a bargain. The captain took
me on board his vessel and made a cook of me. I stayed with
him about two years, and most of the time he treated me
very cruelly. He used to strip and whip me with the cat-o'-
nine-tails. [This cat-o'-nine tails was a rope having nine
long ends and at each end a hard knot.]

One day as we lay at the dock in Richmond, Va., he rose
very early one morning, and told me that he was going up
town, advising me to have breakfast ready by the time he
arrived. The weather was very cold. As it stormed that
morning very hard, I asked him if I could cook down in the

cabin. His reply was "No:" and that I must cook in the caboose. [This caboose was a large black kettle set on the deck, all open to the weather, to make fire in, and supported by bricks to prevent it burning the deck.] Seeing I had to be reconciled to my situation, I made my fire the best I could. The rain and wind extinguished the fire, so that I could not fry the fish; hence I could not turn them, for they cleaved to the frying pan; so I thought I would stir them up in a mess and make poached fish of them; I then poured them out into a dish, and placed them on the table.

Very soon the captain came aboard drunk, and asked me if breakfast was ready; I told him: "Yes." When he went down into the cabin and sat at the table, I crept off and peeped through the cabin window, to see what effect the breakfast would have upon him. While he sat there, I beheld that he looked at the poached fish with a great deal of dissatisfaction and disgust. He called me "doctor," and commanded me to come down into the cabin. I replied promptly. When I got there, he pointed to the fish, and asked me if I could tell which parts of those fish belonged to each other; I told him I could not tell. As the cooking devolved on me that morning, I tried to justify myself by telling him that the rain and wind cooled my pan so that I could not fry the fish, and that I had done the best I could.

After hearing this, he told me to strip myself, and then go and stand on deck till he had eaten his breakfast. I suffered intensely with the cold. Some of the people on the dock laughed at me, while others pitied me. There I was, divested of my clothing! He turned his fiery eyes on me when he came on deck; and, with a look of fierce decision on his face, (for now all the fierceness of his nature was roused), he took a rope's end and applied it vigorously to my naked back until he deemed that I had atoned for my offence. The blows fell hard and fast, raising the skin at every stroke; by the time he was through whipping me I was warm enough. I then went down into the cabin to remove the breakfast things. I did not eat anything, for I had lost all appetite for food. In the course of the day we got under way, and started for home.

We then proceeded down the James River, and thence to a place called Carter's Creek. Here we took in a haul of oysters, and then started for Alexandria. The wind headed us off for several days, and the weather was very cold. At last the wind favored us, enabling us to continue our voyage till we arrived at Chesapeake Bay; just at this time the wind came in contact with our vessel and headed us off again. It was now in the stillness of the night (mid-night) when the mate in the cabin was far under the influence of liquor; he was so beastly drunk that he could not get out to give any assistance whatever. Hence I had to manage the sails the best I could, while the captain stood at the helm. We strove all night endeavoring to get up the bay. About two o'clock in the morning the captain told me to bring up the jug of whisky to him. Just at this time the vessel sprung a leak. I did all I could to stop the leakage: the captain told me to go to the pump and do the best I could till morning. Both of us tried to get the mate out, but did not succeed. We then turned the vessel around and put back, reaching about day the place from whence we first started. By this time the mate was nearly over his drunken spell and was somewhat more sober, seeing what peril we were in, went with us to the pump to free the vessel. On account of the cold weather, we lay in Carter's Creek several days; our oysters spoiled and we were obliged to throw them overboard. We then took in a freight of merchandise and started for Fredericksburg; here we discharged our freight and returned, going down the

Rappahannock we stopped to take in a freight of corn for Fredericksburg. One morning the captain and mate went ashore after a load of corn, leaving me on board to get breakfast and to have it ready by the time they returned. I had it ready as he requested. When they had nearly finished their meal the captain asked me for more tea; I told him it was all out; he wanted to know why I did not make more tea; I told him I thought there was a plenty, it was as much as I generally made. He challenged me for daring to think; he told me to go forward and divest myself of every article of clothing, and wait till he came. When he did come he put my head between his legs, and while I was in this position I thought my last days had come; I thought while he was using the cat-o'-nine tails to my naked back, and hearing the whizzing of the rope, that if ever I got away I would throw myself overboard and put an end to my life. The captain had punished me so much that I was tired of life, for it became a burden to me.

The cat-o'-nine tails had no rest, for so dearly did he love its music that a day seldom passed on which he could find no occasion for its use. On the impulse of the moment, I gave a sudden spring, and struck the water some distance from the vessel, and as I could not swim I began to sink. I found that unless I was helped soon I would drown. I began to repent of what I had done, and wished that I had not committed such a rash act. When I attempted to bring myself up to the surface of the water with success, I looked towards the vessel to see if the captain was coming to help me, and at this moment of my peril, instead of rendering any assistance he sat perfectly at ease, or composed on the deck looking at me, but making no effort to help me. I said to myself, I wonder if that old devil intends to let me drown, and not try to save me. All that I could do I was not able to keep myself on the surface of the water. Before I was out of reach and began to sink for the last time, I felt something grasp me; I found that it was the captain, who finally consented to draw me up to the surface of the water and throw me in the boat. I was so exhausted that I could neither stand up or sit down, but was obliged to lay on the bottom of the boat. While I was lying down he commenced beating me with the cat-o'-nine-tails very unmercifully; the more he beat me, the more the water poured out of my mouth. The mate told me afterwards that the water flowing out of my mouth reminded him of a whale spouting water.

We then pursued our course to Fredericksburg; when reaching there we discharged our merchandise—the vessel made water very fast, so we returned to Carter's Creek to undergo repairs. Here it lay for a number of days, for the ship-carpenters were not ready to take care of her: hence I had to stay by the vessel while the captain and mate went home. After I had been there a few weeks, I sought an opportunity to run away. I saw a vessel one day going to my former home, Mr. Dick. Mitchell's, I got on board this vessel for home, having been gone for two years. I remained at this home about a year and did chores about the house while I did stay, and during the cotton season I had just so much cotton to pick out during the day.

One spring Mr. Mitchell put me in the field to attend to the crows, to prevent them pulling up the corn. This was three or fours years before Mrs. Mitchell's death. This exercise did very well during the week days, but when the Sabbath day came I desired a respite from this monotonous work. The Sabbath day was a lonesome day to me, because the field hands were away that day; the boys would be away frolicking at some place they had chosen. I resolved that I would break up, or put an end to my Sunday employment;

so I studied a plan, while I sat down in the field one Sabbath, how I should accomplish it. First, I thought I would feign sickness; then I said to myself, that will not do, for they will give me something that will physic me to death. My next contrivance was that I would pretend that I had the stomach ache; then, I said again, that will not do either, for then my mistress will make me drunk with whisky, as she had done before by her repeated doses. I devised another scheme, I thought the best of all, and that was to pretend that I had broken my leg again. As this plan was satisfactory to my mind, I arose from where I was sitting and resumed my work. Monday morning I returned to the field, as usual.

All at once I intentionally struck my foot against a stone. I made out that I had broken my leg again. When I came to the house, Jinny, the cook, saw me; her first exclamation was: "Why, chile, what is de matter?" In reply, I only gave a deep, mournful sound, and made a dreadful time about my leg, how it pained me, and so on. The cook, after looking pitifully at me, took my hand and helped me into the kitchen; while there I gave a sad account about my leg; I complained of feeling faint, and desired something to drink that I might feel better. She took a blanket into the adjoining room, and invited me to lie down on the floor. [This adjoining room was a little bedroom attached to the kitchen]. Every effort I made towards lying down I would groan piteously, and whimper as though it hurt me dreadfully. While I was on the floor Mr. Mitchell and the family were at breakfast in the "great house."

Alfred, the servant boy, carried the news to the family that I had broken my leg. As soon as Mr. Mitchell heard of this, he said, with an oath, that he would tend to it when he had eaten his breakfast. It was not long before I heard his speedy steps, as he was coming towards me; just this moment, I said to myself; this day it is either victory or death.

As he stepped into the kitchen he called out to Jinny, the cook, "Where is that one-legged son of a b——?" She replied that I was in the adjoining room, very badly hurt. He, with an awful oath, said that he would break my other leg. When he came into the bedroom where I was he sang out with a loud voice, and, with a dreadful oath, commanding me to rise, or else he would take every inch of skin off from my back. I told him that I was so much hurt that I could not get up. My complaints only vexed him the more, so much so that he told Alfred to go into the house and bring him the rawhide, and said that he would raise me.

By the time the boy had returned, I was up on one leg choking down the sobs now and then. Mr. Mitchell told me to take some corn and replant those hills I had allowed the crows to pull up. I took the corn and started to do my work, groaning and crying at every step; I did not get far before he called me back and asked me if I had eaten my breakfast; I told him I had not. As his passions had subsided, he told me to get my breakfast and then go out and plant the corn. I first went into the kitchen, and then to my room to lie down on the floor. Jinny came to me and asked me if I would have something to eat; I told her I was in too much pain to eat. (Just that moment I was so hungry that I could have eaten the flesh of a dead horse.) After Mrs. Mitchell had removed the breakfast things she came into the kitchen to see how I was, and found me groaning at a great rate, as if in great distress. She put her arm under my head to raise me, for I pretended that I was in so much pain that I could not raise myself.

Mrs. Mitchell was a very tyrannical woman, but notwithstanding her many failings she occasionally manifested a little kindness. She rolled up my pantaloons and commenced bathing my knee with opodeldoc (a sapona-

ceous camphorated liniment) that she used for such purposes; after which she bound it up nicely and then laid me
down again. Mr. Mitchell never came after me any more.
Mrs. Mitchell rebuked her husband by telling him that he
had no business to send me out in the field among the
stumps to attend to the crows, for I was not able to be there.

I lay on the floor in my room about two weeks. In the
course of the afternoon Jinny came into my room and asked
me if I would have something to eat; I told her I would try
and eat a little something, (just then I was hungry enough
to eat a peck). When she returned with some bacon and
corn-cake, (meal cake) I did not dare to eat much for fear
that the rest of the family would mistrust that I was not sick.
At the end of two weeks I asked one of the field hands if the
crows had stopped coming to trouble the corn, his reply
was, "yes, it was so, for the cherries were getting ripe and
they were eating them instead." After hearing this joyful
news I began to grow better very fast. The first day I sat up
nearly all day; the next day I was able to go out some. When
Saturday came I could walk quite a distance to see my
mother, who lived some ten miles off.

Being lame, I was not very profitable on the plantation,
so I went back to live with my mother till she died. At this
time my eldest sister kept house for my father till the
younger children were old enough to be hired out. My
young master had become of age, and had his slaves divided
between himself and his brother, each taking his half. It was
at this time that my young master took me and put me in
charge, or intrusted me to the care of his uncle, in Fairfield,
to learn the shoe-maker's trade. I served four years, during
which time my father died. After I had learned my trade, my
master took me home and opened a shop in Heathsville, Va.,
placing me in it.

*Hired out—Religious experience, conversion—Work as
an exhorter—A slave prayer meeting—Over worked—
A ludicrous accident—Love of dress—Love of freedom—
Death of my master—Religious exercises forbidden—
A stealthy meeting—The surprise—Fairfield Church—
Quarterly meeting—Nancy Merrill—A religious meeting
and a deliverance—Sleeping at my post.*

I ran the shop for one year, during which time my young
master became jealous of me. He thought I was making
more money for myself than for him; it was not so, he was
mistaken about it. What little I did earn for myself was justly
my own. While I was away enjoying myself one Christmas
day, he took an ox-cart with my brother, for Heathsville.
The driving devolved on my brother. My master carried off
my tools and every thing that was in the shop; he hired me
out to a man who was considered by every one to be the
worst one in Heathsville, whose name was Mr. Lacky,
advising him "to keep me very strict, for I was knowing
most too much." I lived with him three years, and managed
so as to escape the cowhide all the time I was there, saving

once. I strove by my prudence and correctness of demeanor to avoid exciting his evil passions. While learning the shoemaker's trade, I was about eighteen years old. At this time I became deeply interested in my soul's salvation; the white people held a prayer meeting in Fairfield one evening in a private house; I attended the meeting that evening, but was not permitted to go in the same room, but only allowed to go in an adjoining room. While there I found peace in believing, and in this happy state of mind I went home rejoicing and praising the Lord for what he had done for me. A few Sabbath's following, I united with the Church in Fairfield. Soon after I was converted I commenced holding meetings among the people, and it was not long before my fame began to spread as an exhorter. I was very zealous, so much so that I used to hold meetings all night, especially if there were any concerned about their immortal soul.

I remember in one instance that having quit work about sundown on a Saturday evening, I prepared to go ten miles to hold a prayer meeting at Sister Gould's. Quite a number assembled in the little cabin, and we continued to sing and pray till daybreak, when it broke. All went to their homes, and I got about an hour's rest while Sister Gould was preparing breakfast. Having partaken of the meal, she, her daughter and myself set out to hold another meeting two miles further; this lasted till about five o'clock, when we returned. Then I had to walk back ten miles to my home, making in all twenty-four miles that day. How I ever did it, lame as I was, I cannot tell, but I was so zealous in the work that I did not mind going any distance to attend a prayer meeting. I actually walked a greater part of the distance fast asleep; I knew the road pretty well. There used to be a great many run-aways in that section, and they would hide away in the woods and swamps, and if they found a person alone as I was, they would spring out at them and rob them. As this thought came into my head during my lonely walk, thinks I, it won't do for me to go to sleep, and I began to look about me for some weapon of defence; I took my jack-knife from my pocket and opened it; now I am ready to stab the first one that tackles me, I said; but try as I would, I commenced to nod, nod, till I was fast asleep again. The long walk and the exertion of carrying on the meeting had nearly used me up.

The way in which we worshipped is almost indescribable. The singing was accompanied by a certain ecstasy of motion, clapping of hands, tossing of heads, which would continue without cessation about half an hour; one would lead off in a kind of recitative style, others joining in the chorus. The old house partook of the ecstasy; it rang with their jubilant shouts, and shook in all its joints. It is not to be wondered at that I fell asleep, for when I awoke I found I had lost my knife, and the fact that I would now have to depend on my own muscle, kept me awake till I had reached the neighborhood of my home. There was a lane about half a mile from the house, on each side of which was a ditch to drain the road, and was nearly half full of water; as I neared this lane I fell asleep again, as the first thing I knew I was in the ditch; I had walked right off into it, best clothes and all. Such a paddling to get out you never saw. I was wide awake enough now you may rest assured, and went into the house sick enough; my feet were all swollen, and I was laid up for two or three days. My mistress came in to see me, and said I must have medicine. I had to bear it, and she dosed me well.

As soon as I was able, I went to work. I had a shop all to myself. My master lived five miles away, but would come once a week and take all the earnings; some weeks I would make a great deal, then I would keep some back for myself,

realized. The master, whose name was Griffin Furshee, had gone to bed, and being awakened by the noise, took his cane and his servant boy and came where the sound directed him. While I was exhorting, all at once the door opened and behold there he stood, with his white face looking in upon us. As soon as I saw the face I stopped suddenly, without even waiting to say amen.

The people were very much frightened; with throbbing hearts some of them went up the log chimney, others broke out through the back door, while a few, who were more self-composed, stood their ground.

When the master came in, he wanted to know what we were doing there, and asked me if I knew that it was against the law for niggers to hold meetings. I expected every moment that he would fly at me with his cane; he did not, but only threatened to report me to my master. He soon left us to ourselves, and this was the last time he disturbed us in our meetings. His object in interrupting us was to find out whether we were plotting some scheme to raise an insurrection among the people. Before this, the white people held a quarterly meeting in the Fairfield Church, commencing Saturday, and continuing eight days and nights without cessation.

The religious excitement that existed at that time was so great that the people did not leave the church for their meals, but had them brought to them. There were many souls converted. The colored people attended every night. The white people occupied the part next to the altar, while the colored people took the part assigned them next to the door, where they held a protracted meeting among themselves. Sometimes, while we were praying, the white people would be singing, and when we were singing they would be praying; each gave full vent to their feelings, yet there was no discord or interruption with the two services. On Wednesday night, the fourth day from the commencement of the meeting, a colored woman by the name of Nancy Merrill, was converted, and when she experienced a change of heart she shouted aloud, rejoicing in the richness of her new found hope. Thursday night, the next evening, the meeting still continued.

By this time the excitement was on the increase among both parties, and it bid fair to hold eight days longer; but right in the midst of the excitement some one came to the door of the church and nodded to the sexton to come to the door; as soon as he did go to the door some one there told him to speak to Nancy Merrill, the new convert, and tell her to come to the door, for he wanted to speak to her. She went, and, behold it was a slave trader, who had bought her during the day from her mistress! As soon as she went to the door, he seized and bound her, and then took her off to her cabin home to get her two boys he had bought also. The sexton came back and reported to us what had taken place.

This thrilling and shocking news sent a sharp shiver through every heart; it went through the church like wildfire; it broke up the meeting entirely among both parties; in less than half an hour every one left the church for home. This woman had a daughter in Fairfield, where I learned my trade, and I hastened home, as soon as possible, to tell the girl what had happened to her mother. She was standing by the fire in the kitchen as I entered—she was the servant girl of John Langsdon, the man who taught me the shoe-maker's trade. As soon as I related to her this sad news she fell to the floor as though she had been shot by a pistol; and, as soon as she had recovered a little from the shock we started for her mother's cabin home, reaching there just in time to see her mother and her two brothers take the vessel for Norfolk, to be sold. This was the last time we ever saw her; we heard, sometime afterwards, that a kind master had bought her, and that she was doing well.

Many thrilling scenes I could relate, if necessary, that makes my blood curdle in my veins while I write. We were treated like cattle, subject to the slave-holders' brutal treatment and law.

The wretched condition of the male slave is bad enough; but that of the woman, driven to unremitting, unrequited toil, suffering, sick, and bearing the peculiar burdens of her own sex, unpitied, not assisted, as well as the toils which belong to another, must arouse the spirit of sympathy in every heart not dead to all feeling. Oh! how many heart-rending prayers I have heard ascend up to the throne of grace for deliverance from such exhibitions of barbarity. How many family ties have been broken by the cruel hand of slavery. The priceless store of pleasures, and the associations connected with home were unknown to the doomed slaves, for in an unlooked for hour they were sold to be separated from father and mother, brothers and sisters. Oh! how many such partings have rent many a heart, causing it to bleed as it were, and crushing out all hope of ever seeing slavery abolished.

Sometime before I left for the north, the land of freedom, I appointed another meeting in an off house on a plantation not far from Heathsville, where a number of us collected together to sing and pray. After I had given out the hymn, and prayed, I commenced to exhort the people. While I did so I became very warm and zealous in the work, and perhaps made more noise than we were aware of. The patrolers* going along the road, about half a mile off, heard

---

*The patrolers were southern spies, sent out, or were wont to roam at night to hunt up run-away slaves, and to investigate other matters.

the sound and followed it where we were holding our meeting. They came, armed to the teeth, and surrounded the house. The captain of the company came in, and as soon as we saw him we fell on our knees and prayed that God might deliver us. While we prayed he stood there in the middle of the floor, without saying a word. Pretty soon we saw that his knees began to tremble, for it was too hot for him, so he turned and went out. His comrades asked him if "he was going to make an arrest;" he said "no, it was too hot there for him." They soon left, and that was the last we saw of them.

As God had delivered us in such a powerful manner, we took courage and held our meeting until day-break. Another time I had a meeting appointed at a freed-woman's house, whose name was Sister Gouldman, about five miles in the country. I left home about seven o'clock on Saturday evening, and arrived there about ten; we immediately commenced the meeting and continued it till about daylight. After closing the meeting we slept while Sister Gouldman was preparing the breakfast. After breakfast we went two miles further, and held another meeting till late in the afternoon, then closed and started for home, reaching there some time during the night. I was very much fatigued, and my energies were entirely exhausted, so much so that I was not able to work the next day.

The time when I was eighteen years old, when such a miraculous change had been wrought in my heart, I had had two holidays, and was up all night holding meetings, praying and singing most of the time. Not having any sleep, I could scarcely keep my eyes open when I went to work. While endeavoring to finish a piece of work, Mr. Lacky came and found me asleep while I was on my bench shoe-making. He told me that I had "been away enjoying myself for two days, and if he should come again and find me asleep, he would wake me up." Sure enough, he had no sooner left the shop when I was fast asleep again. As his shop was beneath mine, he could easily hear me when I was at work. He came up again in his stocking-feet, unawares, and the first thing I knew he had the rawhide, applying it vigorously to my flesh in such a manner that did not feel very pleasant to me. After punishing me, he asked me "if I thought I could keep awake after this." I told him "I thought possibly I could," and did, through a great deal of effort till night. I never was satisfied about that whipping.

ESCAPE
FROM SLAVERY

Near the end of the third year I went to my young master and told him I did not care about living with Mr. Lacky any longer. He told me that I could choose for myself another man whom I could live with. I concluded to live with one by the name of Bailey, who did not strike me during the year, but threatened to, which made me mad. About the end of this time I thought very strongly in reference to freedom, liberty; the precious goal which I almost grasped. I pursued daily my humble duties, waiting with patience till I could perceive some opening in the dense dark cloud that enveloped my fate in the hidden future. Before I lived with Bailey, I had some thought of this. I became acquainted with a man by the name of Zip, who was a sailor; I told him my object in reference to freedom. He told me that he also was intending to make his escape and to have his freedom. This was in the year 1836. We agreed that whenever there was a chance we would come off together. About Christmas, 1837, we made an arrangement to run away. Zip was calculating to take the vessel that the white people had left during their absence. He was left to take care of this vessel till they returned; nevertheless he intended to use it to a good purpose, for he took this opportunity to make his escape. We intended to carry off seventy, but we were disappointed because we could not carry out our arrangements. It was a very cold Christmas Eve, so much so that the river was badly frozen, not making it favorable for us to capture her: hence we gave that project up until the spring of 1838.

On the 6th day of May, 1838, Zip, with another one by the name of Lorenzo and myself, each hired a horse to take a short journey up the country to Lancaster, to see a sick friend of ours, who was very ill, for we did not expect to see him again. His name was Lewis Vollin. We had calculated to make our escape in about two weeks; so we started one Sabbath morning and found our friend quite sick, and was only able to sit up a little while and talk with us. Lewis' doctor was an aged colored man, who was a fortune-teller also, and could unfold the past, present, and future destiny of any one. Our sick friend was at this doctor's home, for the purpose of being cured by him. While there, the doctor asked us to walk out and look at his place; we did so, and after a while we sat down under a large tree. The doctor then asked us if we would like to have our fortune's told; we told him "yes." He sent to the house for his cards, and after receiving them, told each of us to cut them; we did so, then he took my cut and looked it over, saying, "you are going to run away; I see that you will have good luck; you will go clear; you will reach the free country in safety; you will gather many friends around you, both white and colored; you will be worth property, and in the course of time will return back home, and walk over your native land." I asked him "how that could be; was I to be captured and brought back?" He said, "no, you will come back because you wish to, and go away again." I told him "that was something that I did not understand." He said, "nevertheless, it is so."

He then told the fortunes of my two companions, Zip and Lorenzo. He examined their cuts, and said they would all go clear; but never said they would return, neither did they, for they died before freedom was proclaimed. Zip died at the West Indies, Lorenzo died on the ship in some port at the time the cholera broke out.

In the afternoon we started for home, reaching there about four o'clock. When we reached Heathsville, the place where we lived, we noticed as we rode up to the stable to put the horses away, (for we were on horse-back) that there were half a dozen or more young men, who appeared to be talking and whittling behind the stable. The stable where I put my horse was on one side of the street, and the stable where Zip was to put his was on the opposite side. Zip went up to the door to put his horse in, but found that it would not open readily, and while he was trying to open it those white young men whom we saw whittling, supposing that he had got in, began to assemble around the door. Now among these young men was a negro-trader who spoke to Zip, asking him "why he did not go in and put the horse away." Zip told him that "he could not get the door open." The trader then took hold of the door and it came open immediately. Zip was so astonished to think that the door opened so readily to the negro-trader, and did not yield to him, that he thought there must be something wrong about it. He refused to go in himself, and only fastened the horse's bridle to a fence, then went over to the tavern to tell the hostler that he might put the horse away. From there he went to his house, for he lived there in town, and as soon as he entered the house his wife warned him to flee for his life, for a trader had bought him, and had been to the house with several young men whom we saw behind the stable as we rode up, placed themselves there for the purpose of waiting till we came. Their motive was, when Zip went into the stable to close the door on him and capture him.

I knew nothing about this at the time. I put my horse away, went to the house, got something to eat, then started to go off some five miles to see some friends; but before I started I thought I would go into my shop and brush my coat; while there I sat down on my bench just for a few moments, and all at once I fell asleep. When I awoke the sun was just going down. I think I had been asleep about an hour. I did not have any idea of falling asleep when I entered the shop, for I intended to have gone out of town. As quick as thought I jumped up, took my hat and started for the door; just as I opened it there was a man passing by whose name was Griffin Muse, who belonged on James Smith's plantation about two miles off. He saw me as I opened the door, and said to me, "Lindsey, where have you been? I have been looking for you this two hours. I just started to go down home and give up the search, and to tell Zip that I could not find you." Said I, "what is the matter?" Said he to me, "did you not know that Zip was sold to a Georgian trader, who is trying to catch him." Said I, "where is Zip?" I am sure I did not know anything about this, I did not dream of such a thing; I saw this trader, with some young men behind the stable, but did not dream that he was after Zip. Griffin Muse said to me, "Zip is down on our plantation, and has sent me after you, and that his intention is to try to make his escape to-night to a free country, and if you are going with him to go to him as soon as possible." I was so astonished that I did not know what to do. I told him to "wait for me, and I would get ready as soon as possible." I went a few blocks where I kept my box, and in it I had three dollars, all the money I possessed in the world. On my way back I met a man who owed me fifty cents; I dunned him, and as good luck would have it he had the money and paid me.

I then went back to my shop and picked up all the things that I thought I would want to take with me. While I was making my arrangements my boss came into the shop. As soon as I saw him coming I pushed my bundle under the bench and sat down on the bench, pretending to be sick. He asked me if I "was going to church," I told him I thought "I should not, for I was not feeling very well." After a while he went out and closed the door after him. Soon as he was gone I finished gathering up my things, then locked up the shop and went into the "great house" to put the key over the mantle-piece. Then Griffin Muse, Zip's wife and myself started for Smith's plantation, about two miles from Heathsville, where Zip was secreted.

When we arrived there Zip and Lorenzo were just starting; it was nearly eleven o'clock; they had waited for me till they thought I was not coming. They were just bidding the folks farewell as I arrived at the house where Zip stopped.★ Two minutes more and I would have been left behind. If I had not fallen asleep in the shop I would have been out of town, and I should have been left, for Griffin

★These were Zip's plantation friends that were at this cabin home.

would not have found me; and if I had slept one minute longer he would have passed by the shop and I would not have seen him: one minute more, either way, would have turned the scales.

All three of us, Zip, Lorenzo and myself, assembled together and started for the Cone River, about a quarter of a mile from where we were. There were a number of our plantation friends who went with us; Zip's wife and her mother, and a number of others. When we came to the river, we stood on the beach and embraced, kissed, and bade each other farewell. The scene between Zip and his wife at parting was distressing to behold. Oh! how the sobbing of his wife resounded in the depths of his heart; we could not take her with us for the boat was too small.

In the first place we took a small canoe and crossed the river till we came to a plantation owned by a man named Travis. He had a large sail boat that we desired to capture, but we did not know how we should accomplish it, as they took a great deal of pains generally to haul her up, lock her up and put the sails and oars in the barn. As it was the Sabbath day, the young folk had been sailing about the river, and instead of securing her as they usually did, they left her anchored in the stream with the sails and oars all in the boat. This was very fortunate for us, for the house was very near to the shore, besides they had very savage dogs there. So it would have been a very difficult matter for us to attempt to capture the boat sails and oars if they had been where they were generally kept. So all we had to do was to run our canoe along side the boat and get on board.

It was quite calm before we started, but as soon as we got ready, and the sails set, the wind began to rise, and all that night we had all the wind we could carry sail to. Lorenzo and myself, by keeping our oars in motion, outran everything that stayed on the water. By the next morning we were a great distance from home. We sailed all day and night Monday, and until Tuesday night about nine o'clock, when we landed just below Frenchtown, Maryland. We there hauled the boat up the best we could, and fastened her, then took our bundles and started on foot. Zip, who had been a sailor from a boy, knew the country and understood where to go. He was afraid to go through Frenchtown, so we took a circuitous route, until we came to the road that leads from Frenchtown to New Castle. Here I became so exhausted that I was obliged to rest; we went into the woods, which were near by, and laid down on the ground and slept for an hour or so, then we started for New Castle.

I found I could not keep up with my companions, for they could walk much faster than myself, and hence got far ahead, and then would have to wait for me; I being lame was not able to keep up with them. At last Zip said to me, "Lindsey, we shall have to leave you for our enemies are after us, and if we wait for you we shall all be taken; so it would be better for one to be taken than all three." So after he had advised me what course to take, they started, and in a few minutes left me out of sight. When I had lost sight of them, I sat down by the road-side and wept, prayed, and wished myself back where I first started. I thought it was all over with me forever; I thought one while I would turn back as far as Frenchtown, and give myself up to be captured; then I thought that would not do; a voice spoke to me, "not to make a fool of myself, you have got so far from home, (about two hundred and fifty miles), keep on towards freedom, and if you are taken, let it be heading towards freedom." I then took fresh courage and pressed my way onward towards the north with anxious heart.

It was then two or three o'clock Wednesday morning,

the 8th of May. I came to the portion of the road that had been cut through a very high hill, called the "deep cut," which was in a curve, or which formed a curve; when I had got about mid-way of this curve I heard a rumbling sound that seemed to me like thunder; it was very dark, and I was afraid that we were to have a storm; but this rumbling kept on and did not cease as thunder does, until at last my hair on my head began to rise; I thought the world was coming to the end. I flew around and asked myself, "what is it?" At last it came so near to me it seemed as if I could feel the earth shake from under me, till at last the engine came around the curve. I got sight of the fire and the smoke; said I, "it's the devil, it's the devil!" It was the first engine I had ever seen or heard of; I did not know there was anything of the kind in the world, and being in the night, made it seem a great deal worse than it was; I thought my last days had come; I shook from head to foot as the monster came rushing on towards me. The bank was very steep near where I was standing; a voice says to me, "Fly up the bank;" I made a desperate effort, and by the aid of the bushes and trees which I grasped, I reached the top of the bank, where there was a fence; I rolled over the fence and fell to the ground, and the last words I remember saying were, that "the devil is about to burn me up. farewell! farewell!" After uttering these words I fainted, or as I expressed it, I lost myself.

I do not know how long I lay there, but when I had recovered, (or came to myself), the devil had gone. Oh! how my heart did throb; I thought the patrollers were after me on horseback. After I had gathered strength enough I got up and sat there thinking what to do; I first thought I would go off to the woods somewhere and hide myself till the next night, and then pursue my journey onward; but then I thought that would not do, for my enemies, who were pur-

"I Made a Desperate Effort."—*Page* 44.

suing me, would overtake and capture me. So I made up my mind that I would not loose any more time than was necessary; hence I crawled down the bank and started on with trembling steps, expecting every moment that that monster would be coming back to look for me.

Thus between hope, and fear, and doubt, I continued on foot till at last the day dawned and the sun had just began to rise. When the sun had risen as high as the tops of the trees, the monster all at once was coming back to meet me; I said to myself, "it is no use to run, I had just as well stand and make the best of it," thinking I would make the best bargain that I could with his majesty. Onward he came, with smoke and fire flying, and as he drew near to me, I exclaimed to myself, "why! what a monster's head he has on to him." Oh! said I, "look at his tushes,* I am a goner;" I looked again, saying to myself, "look at the wagons he has tied to him." Thinks I, "they are the wagons that he carries the souls to hell with." I looked through the windows to see if I could see any black people that he was carrying, but I did not see one, nothing but white people. Then I thought it was not black people that he was after, but only the whites, and I did not care how many of them he took. He went by me like a flash; I expected every moment that he would stop and bid me come aboard, (for I had been a great hand to abuse the old gentleman; when at home I use to preach against him), but he did not, so I thought that he was going so fast he could not stop. He was soon out of sight, and I for the first time took a long breath.

I was very hungry, for I had not eaten anything much for days. We came away in such a hurry that we did not have time to prepare much food; we took only some corn-cake and a little bacon; I was almost starved to death; I became quite weak, and looked around on the ground to see if I

---

*The cow-catcher in front of the engine.

could find anything green that I could eat. I began to fail very fast, I thought I should die there on the road. All at once I came to a house, and a voice seemed to say to me, "go to that house and see if you can get something to eat." I said to myself, "there are white people that live there and I shall be captured. They can but capture me, and if I stay away I shall die." I went up to the door and rapped; a lady came to the door and looked at me with a smile upon her countenance as I spoke to her. I said to myself, "I do not mind you white people's smiles, I expect you think to make money off of me this morning." I asked her if "she would give me something to eat." She said, "she had nothing cooked, but if I would come in she would get me something." I thought to myself, "I know what that means, you want me to come in in order to capture me;" but nevertheless I went in, and she set a chair up to the fire-place and bade me sit down. Her husband sat there in one corner, and looking up said to me: "My man, you are traveling early this morning," I said, "yes, I made an early start." (I did not tell him I had been traveling all day and all night for three nights.) He asked me "how far I was going," I told him "I was going to Philadelphia; that I had some friends there whom I had not seen for some time, and I was going to visit them, and then return in a few weeks." Very soon his wife had my breakfast all ready of ham, eggs, and a meal-cake, and put them on the table, and then asked me to sit down. I did so, without waiting for a second invitation, and the first mouthful I took seemed to me as if it would go straight through me; I ate till I became alarmed, for I thought I would betray myself by my eating. I ate up most everything she put on the table, then I got up and asked, "what I should pay for my breakfast," she said, "twenty-five cents." I put my hand in my pocket and picked out a quarter, giving it to her. I started on my journey, feeling like a new man. I walked on till about noon, at which time I reached New Castle. The first one I saw was Lorenzo, who was one of the men who left me on the road. He came a little way out of the city to look for me, to see if I was any where in sight; we met and went into the city, found Zip, and once more we were together. The boat left there for Philadelphia twice a day. She had left in the morning before they had arrived, but she returned in the afternoon, only to start right off again the same afternoon.

By the time the boat had returned, I was there, so we three all went on board. How we ever passed through New Castle as we did, without being detected, is more than I can tell, for it was one of the worst slave towns in the country, and the law was such that no steamboat, or anything else, could take a colored person to Philadelphia without first proving his or her freedom. What makes it so astonishing to me is, that we walked aboard right in sight of every body, and no one spoke a word to us. We went to the captain's office and bought our tickets, without a word being said to us.

We arrived safely in Philadelphia that afternoon; there upon the wharf we separated, after bidding each other farewell. Lorenzo and Zip went on board a ship for Europe, and went to sea. I started up the street, not knowing where I was going, or what would become of me; I walked on till I came to a shoe store, went in and asked a white gentleman, "do you want to hire a shoe-maker?" He said, "I do not, but think you can find a place by going a little further." I proceeded a little further, and came to a shop kept by a colored man, whose name was Simpson. I went in and introduced myself to him the best I could. (I did not let him know that I was a fugitive.) We sat there and talked till most night; I then asked him if he "could keep me all night?" He replied, "no, for it was not convenient for him to do so."

Here I was, hedged in, not knowing what course to take; I was down cast, and the thought of having no friend or shelter only sank me into deeper perplexity. He told me "he had a brother who lived on a certain street, who he thought would take me." Hearing this I felt somewhat encouraged, but not understanding the number he gave me, in order to find his brother, I was as badly off as before. As it was getting late he began to make preparation for shutting up his shop. My heart began to ache within me, for I was puzzled what to do; but just before he shut up, a colored minister came in; I thought perhaps I could find a friend in him, and when he was through talking with Simpson he started to go out, I followed him to the side-walk and asked him "if he would be kind enough to give me lodging that night." He told me "he could not, for he was going to church; that it would be late before the service closed, and besides it would not be convenient for him."

Here the same heavy cloud closed in upon me again, for it was getting dark, and I had no where to sleep that night. Circumstances were against me; he told me "I could get a lodging place if I would go to the tavern." I made no reply to this advice, but felt somewhat sad, for my last hope had fled. He then asked me if "I was free." I told him that "I was a free man." (I did not intend to let him know that I was a fugitive.) Here I was in a great dilemma, not knowing what to do or say. He told me if "I was a fugitive I would find friends." "If any one needs a friend I do," thought I to myself, for just at this time I needed the consolation and assistance of a friend, one on whom I could rely. So thought I, "it will be best for me to make known that I am a fugitive, and not to keep it a secret any longer." I told him frankly that "I was from the South, and that I was a runaway." He said, "you are;" I said "yes." He asked me if I "had told Simpson;" I said "no." He then called Simpson and asked him "if he knew that this brother was a fugitive," He said "no." After finding this to be a fact, Simpson asked me if "that was so?" I said "it was." He then told me to "come with him, that he had room enough for me." I went home with him and he introduced me to his family, and they all had a great time rejoicing over me. After giving me a good supper, they secreted me in a little room called the fugitive's room, to sleep; I soon forgot all that occurred around me. I was resting quietly in the arms of sleep, for I was very tired.

The next morning Simpson went in pursuit of the two men who had been with me, but he could not find them. I have never seen them since. My parting with them at the Philadelphia wharf was the last I saw of them. Simpson then went among the Abolitionists, and informed them of my case; many of them came to see me. They talked of sending me to England; one Quaker asked me if I would like "to see the Queen." I told him that "I did not care where I went so long as I was safe." They held a meeting that day, and decided to send me to Springfield, Mass.; this was the fifth day after I left home. The next day, Friday morning, Brother Simpson took me down to the steamboat and started me for New York, giving me a letter directed to David Ruggles, of New York.

The nearer I came to New York the worse I felt, for I did not know how I should find Mr. Ruggles. Just as I reached the dock there was a lady whom I had never seen before; I went to her and asked her "if she knew of such a man, by the name of David Ruggles?" She told me that she "did know of such a person, and that he lived on her way home." She kindly consented to show me where he lived. I went along with her without any more trouble in mind about it. I gave Ruggles the letter, and we had a great time rejoicing together. I stayed with him till Monday. On

Monday, the ninth day of my travels, he gave me two letters, one to a Mr. Foster, in Hartford; and the other to Doctor Osgood, in Springfield. Mr. Ruggles sent a boy with me down to the steamboat, and I started for Hartford on a boat which sailed in the afternoon.

Towards night I went up to the clerk's office to pay my fare. I asked him "how much it would be?" He told me it was "three dollars." I told him it was a large sum of money, more than I possessed." He then asked me "how much I had?" I told him "two dollars and fifty-eight cents." He told me that "that would not do, and that I must get the rest of it." I told him "that I was a stranger there, and that I knew no one." He said: "You should have asked and found out." I told him "I did, and was told that the fare would be two dollars, and that was nearly all I possessed at that time." He requested me to hand it to him, which I did, and it robbed me of every cent I had. I then took my ticket and went forward and laid down among some bales of cotton. It was very chilly and cold, and I felt very much depressed in spirits and cast down.

The climate had changed much since I left home, I was out of money and among strangers; my heart sank within me, for I was faint and hungry, and had no means to pay for my supper. I fell asleep while lying among the bales of cotton. After tea was over with the passengers, one of the waiters came and awoke me, and asked if "I wanted any supper?" I replied "no," knowing that I had no means to pay for it. Soon another one came and cordially invited me to partake of some, that it would cost me nothing. I went to the cabin, and had an excellent supper. The old saying proved true in my case, that "a friend in need is a friend in deed." Before I retired for the night, some one came through the cabin and told the way-passengers that they must come to the captain's office and leave the number of their berth before they retired for the night. I did not know what he meant by that saying; I thought it meant all the passengers to pay extra for their berths. Now, thought I, if that is the case, and I sleep in the berth all night, and in the morning have no money to pay with, I shall be in trouble sure enough. As I was very tired, I desired very much to lie down and rest; so I thought I would risk it and lie down and sleep till daylight. I reached Hartford quite early the next morning, so I lay till I thought the boat was along-side the wharf; I then got up and dressed myself and looked at the number of my berth, as I was told to see what it was, so if I should meet the captain I could tell him. I then started for the deck, and on reaching there I looked around, and wondered how I should find Mr. Foster. While I was looking, I saw a colored man standing, and seemed to be looking at me; I went up to him and asked him if "he knew a man by the name of Foster?" He replied: "Yes." I asked him if he would show me where he lived? He said: "Yes." So he went along with me, and I found Mr. Foster's residence, by direction given; and, finding him at home, I presented the letter. After he had read it, he began to congratulate me on my escape. When he had conversed with me awhile, he went out among the friends, (Abolitionists), and informed them of my circumstances, in order to solicit aid to forward me on to Springfield.

Many of them came in to see me, and received me cordially; I began to realize that I had some friends. I stayed with Mr. Foster till afternoon. He raised three dollars for my benefit and gave it to me, and then took me to the steamboat and started me for Springfield. I reached there a little before night.

When I had reached the wharf I stepped ashore, and saw a man standing on the dock; and, after inquiries concerning

Doctor Osgood's residence, he kindly showed it to me. The Doctor, being at home, I gave him the letter, and as soon as he had read it, he and his family congratulated me on my escape from the hand of the oppressor. He informed me that the letter stated "that he could either send me to Canada, or he could keep me in Springfield, just as he thought best." He said: "I think we will keep you here, so you can make yourself a home." The family gathered around me to listen to my thrilling narrative of escape. We talked till the bell notified them that supper was ready. An excellent meal was prepared for me, which I accepted gladly, for the Doctor was a very liberal man, saying: "Friend, come in and have some supper."

Wheat bread was the same as cake to me in those days, for my food at the South was principally corncake and bacon. While I was eating, his daughter said: "Don't be afraid, but help yourself." Not being accustomed to eating at the "great house" at home, you must imagine that it produced some embarrassment in my mind. When the supper was over, the family gathered in the sitting-room for prayers, as it was their custom to read a portion of the Scriptures before retiring for the night; and I was asked to read with them. Before conducting prayers the Doctor sang one of his favorite hymns, in which all the family united. I listened with pleasure, and my whole soul entered into the holy service.

The next morning the Doctor asked me "how I rested?" I replied, "very well sir." He informed me that breakfast would soon be ready. It was customary for them to have prayers before the morning meal, which was something new to me; it seemed more like a meeting to me, to attend prayers with such a pious family. Dr. Osgood was very benevolent, and his charitable deeds were many; none were turned away hungry from his door. I was much impressed with his genial spirit, consistent and zealous piety, and activity in the cause of Christ. His life was upright, pure, and good, and his Christian faith unfaltering. None in want ever appealed to him in vain. Truly that passage of Scripture can be applied to him, "For I was an hungered and ye gave me meat: I was thirsty and ye gave me drink: I was a stranger and ye took me in: Naked and ye clothed me: I was sick and ye visited me: I was in prison and ye came unto me." "Verily I say unto you inasmuch as ye have done it unto one of the least of these my brethren, ye have done it unto me."

Rev. Dr. Osgood who "always abounded in the works of the Lord," was in the habit of rising very early, and held prayer meetings twice a week, from five to six o'clock in the morning. The young and the aged gathered at the chapel, which was half-a-mile from the Doctor's residence. The day laborers who "earned their bread by the sweat of their brow," attended before going to work; also, the wealthy were there, and it was an hour of refreshing to many souls. The invigorating air of the early morning seemed to make the conference room a fitting place for the holy spirit.

The opening hymn was most generally sung, beginning thus:

"Lord, in the morning thou shalt hear
    My voice ascending high:
To Thee will I direct my prayer,
    To Thee lift up mine eye.

"Up to the hills where Christ is gone,
    To plead for all His saints,
Presenting at His Father's throne
    Our songs and our complaints."

★　★　★　★　★　★　★

Which echoed beautifully as the birds sang in the spring their sweetest carols, as they flew among the branches of the large elm tree which stood before the door of the chapel. All were very devotional, unlike as it is with us, for every one bowed the head in silent prayer as they entered the house of God, and really it did seem like a heaven below.

Dr. Osgood was pastor over a large congregation. His church was a large, white Presbyterian church, on a beautiful green lawn not far from the chapel. The early morning services resulted in a large revival, in which one hundred came out on the Lord's side, rejoicing in their new-found hopes. All were made welcome, and Christian fellowship was truly exhibited towards all.

V | LIFE IN FREEDOM

*Employment in a shoe shop—Education at Wilbraham—
Licensed to preach—John M. Brown—Mrs. Cecelia
Platt—Elizabeth Osgood—Sabbath and Mission
Schools—Return to Springfield—Engagement with Dr.
Hudson—Experience at Saybrook—Persecutions of
Abolitionists—Lecturing—Courtship and marriage.*

Dr. Osgood felt an interest in my safety, for my master was on my track, and had advertised me through the press, trying every means to get me, if possible. The Doctor secreted me in a little room, called the fugitive's room. As I was secreted, all schemes to capture were baffled.

After keeping me for a while, the Doctor endeavored to find employment for me as a shoe-maker. He went to several persons, but found none that would take me. Finally, for safety—and the last resort—he went to see Mr. Elmore, an Abolitionist, who was a wholesale shoe dealer on Main Street. He readily took me, saying: "Bring him to me, I want to see him." I went to him one night with the Doctor, and he made a bargain with me, and also gave me some work to do in his work-shop, secreted from public gaze. It was the first work I had ever done in the like of a freedman, which gave me strength to think I was a man with others.

I stayed with him one year, and during that year, besides clothing myself and paying my board, I saved one hundred and thirty dollars. I soon became a great favorite with all the hands in the shop. I well knew a man in Springfield who commenced with only six cents in his pocket—for he was once a poor apprentice boy—who, in the course of time became a wealthy man, which gave me great encouragement to save my earnings.

As I never had any advantages for obtaining an education, I felt the importance of it at this time. I made known my desire to Mr. Elmore, who said it was a good project, and advised me to attend school by all means. The old saying is, "it is money that makes the wheels turn, but after all, education moves the locomotive." I then made preparation to attend school at Wilbraham, Mass. After I had been there a while I became quite proficient in my studies, especially in mathematics, it being my favorite study. At first I found it difficult to keep up with the course of study; I overcame it, however, and progressed so rapidly that the students and the faculty of the academy gave me great praise. I remained two or three years. As I was a poor student, I worked at my trade to pay my board and tuition. So many hours were given me for work, and so many for study; and thus I kept myself busily employed while at Wilbraham.

The reason I attended school there was because it was a more retired place for me. I was very ambitious to learn, for I knew I would be better qualified to enter into business for myself, which I had some thoughts of doing then. While I was at Wilbraham I was licensed to preach the Gospel; I held meetings in Springfield and Ludlow, and the Lord blessed me in my endeavors. I had a fellow-student who occupied the same room with me; this chum of mine was a young man from Philadelphia, by the name of John M. Brown, who was then preparing for college. After completing the academical course, he attended Oberlin College, and graduated with honors, and then became professor of Wilberforce College for young men. He expressed a strong desire for me to finish my education at Oberlin, but not having sufficient means to pay my expenses, I did not go.

As we were firm friends, it was sorrowful for us to part, as I found much pleasure in his company. We walked together, spent our hours of recreation together, conversed on themes that interested us the most while we were students at Wilbraham.

In the course of some years he was chosen presiding Bishop of the Methodist Episcopal Churches of color. While at Wilbraham, Mr. Brown and myself held a series of meetings in Springfield, at the house of a Mrs. Cecelia Platt, for the colored people had no church of their own at this time to worship in. Mrs. Platt was a devoted Christian, of many remarkable characteristics, and zealous in the works of the Lord. She long since has been summoned to reap her reward; she died in the triumph of faith. Her house was the welcome home of strangers and friends, whom she always made happy and comfortable. Her home was called the "pastors' home," for they were always made welcome whenever they came. Some of the students, those studying for the ministry, would come in from Wilbraham on Saturdays, and stop at the home of Mrs. Platt, in case of a storm, or being fatigued by the journey, and return on Monday morning. She was very charitable to the needy; as a Christian, very few were her equal. It was there where the first preaching service was held, and the first Sabbath School began. In referring to the Sabbath School, I must acknowledge that those who were engaged in this great work were ardent and active workers, for there were no timid drones.

Mrs. Stebbins—better known as the teacher among the freedmen in the barracks in Washington has since gone to rest from her labors; peacefully fell asleep in Jesus—was one of the most faithful co-workers of this institution.

Miss Elizabeth Osgood, the daughter of Dr. Osgood, was very enthusiastic in this mission; her deeds attracted more than a passing notice, and through her instrumentality many poor children were clothed so as to be presentable for Sabbath School. She went out into the highways and hedges and gathered them in with their tattered garments, with the promise of a new suit of clothes; and thus many a little heart was made glad.

Miss Osgood was then a member of the Washingtonian Society. The object of this society was for the benefit of the poor. Useful articles of all kinds of wearing apparel were made for the needy.

We now turn our thoughts to the Sabbath School. In establishing the school the co-workers took pains, in the course of the week, to notify all the children of the neighborhood, and went out into the lanes and hedges, urging them to come into the proposed school. They were taught Bible truths, thus preparing them for future usefulness. Many of the scholars were newly impressed with something that would go with them through the week, and restrain them from sin; also, keeping them in the fear of God. The influence of the Sunday School was felt in the community. The scholars became interested in the lessons, and loved and respected their instructors. Through the aid of the Presbyterians this school was organized; and, opening with five scholars, the number increased to twenty, and then to one hundred. A small library was procured. A lady aged ninety years, who attended the school, learned to read the Bible, and the perusal of its sacred pages was a great comfort to her.

After awhile, when the school was fully established, we opened a class-meeting, and the parents of the children, and other adults, began to flock to the house of prayer. They came from all quarters to enjoy one another's experiences, feeling it was good for them to be there. As the people came in such numbers, there was not sufficient room in Mrs. Platt's home for the convenience of the people. We found it necessary to build a Chapel near by, and accomplished it within a year's time. It was plainly built, only for temporary use, till we could do better. Before entering it, however, a large revival broke out, which resulted in the conversion of souls.

During the revival I generally made it a point to come in from Wilbraham—a distance of nine miles—Saturday afternoons for the purpose of assisting in the meetings on the Sabbath. Occasionally the white students of Wilbraham Academy would favor me with a pleasant drive in a buggy. Those who had relatives in Springfield often visited them on Saturday. They came to our quarterly and revival meetings, and seemed to take quite an interest in them. They were very enthusiastic, and helped us, by their remarks and testimonies, making the meeting a power for good. Many of the faithful, who sustained these meetings, have long ago been called to the great "Harvest Home," where, I doubt not, there will be gathered many rich and precious sheaves.

At this time the colored ladies of the Chapel resolved to organize a Sewing Society, which consisted of a President, Vice President, Secretary and Treasurer. There was also a committee of ladies who went around to solicit funds to carry out their plans. They had no regular sewing room, but went around from house to house.

After accumulating thirty or forty dollars' worth of sewing, they opened a fair in Masonic Hall; the proceeds were used towards building a more commodious Church for worship. A fair audience attended; the hall was profusely trimmed with evergreens, and the galleries with floral wreathes, intermingled with evergreens, and flags placed at different points. Certain parts of the hall were devoted to the sale of useful articles, which had been generously donated to the ladies by the merchants. There were fancy articles of all descriptions, and the needle-work was finely executed. The ice-cream, lemonade, and pastry were served by competent ladies, who received a liberal patronage. The ladies labored arduously to make the fair a success, and their untiring efforts were well rewarded. The committee received from time to time, sums of money from benevolent persons to encourage them in the great work they had undertaken. God prospered them, and in the course of a few years, a Methodist Church was built on Main Street. Now they have two churches; the second church is on Elm Street.

Many changes have taken place in Springfield; the house where we held our first meeting has long since been completely demolished, and given place to railroad tracks, on which street cars and omnibuses run. In going to Chicopee it looks like a level plain as far as the eye can reach. This village is now a part of Springfield, making it a city of many manufacturing resources, and in consequence is a thrifty and enterprising city. So time changes all things.

Finally I left school and returned to Springfield. I became acquainted with Dr. Hudson, an Abolitionist of great note in those days, who was an anti-slavery lecturer. It was no small thing to be a worker in such a cause. The Doctor engaged me to travel with him for one year; I, according to agreement, accompanied him, for I desired to do all the good I could. We had great success in our mission; we traveled all through the eastern and western part of Connecticut, and a part of Massachusetts. We had some opposition to contend with; it made it much better for the Doctor in having me with him. Brickbats and rotten eggs were very common in those days; an anti-slavery lecturer was often showered by them. Slavery at this time had a great many friends.

When we were in Saybrook there was but one Abolitionist in the place, and whose wife was sick. As we could not be accommodated at his house, we stopped at a tavern; the inmates were very bitter toward us, and more especially to the Doctor. I became much alarmed about my own situation; there was an old sea captain who was there that night, and while in conversation with the Doctor, had some very hard talk, which resulted in a dispute, or contest in words; I thought it would terminate in a fight. The captain asked the Doctor, "what do you know about slavery? All you know about it I suppose, is what this fellow (meaning me) has told you, and if I knew who his master was, and where he was, I would write to him to come on and take him." This frightened me very much; I whispered to the Doctor that we had better retire for the night. We went to our rooms. I feared I should be taken out of my room before morning, so I barred my door with chairs and other furniture that was in the room, before I went to bed. Notwithstanding, I did not sleep much that night. When we had arisen the next morning and dressed ourselves, we went down stairs, but did not stay to breakfast; we took our breakfast at the house of the man whose wife was sick. We gave out notice, by hand-bills, that we would lecture in the afternoon; so we made preparation, and went at the time appointed. The hall was filled to its utmost capacity, but we could not do much, owing to the pressure that was so strong against us: hence we had no success in this place. We went to the tavern and stayed that night. The next morning we went about two miles from this place to the township, and stopped at the house of a friend; one of the same persuasion. He went to the school committee, and got the use of the school-house. We gave out notice that there would be an anti-slavery lecture in the school-house that night. When it was most time for us, word came that we could not have the school-house for the purpose of such a lecture.

We thought that we would not be out-done by obstacles. The man at whose house we were stopping cordially told us that we might have the use of his house; so we changed the place of the lecture from the school-house to his house. The house was full; and we had as we thought, a good meeting. At the close of the lecture the people retired for home. After awhile we retired for the evening, feeling that we had the victory.

The next morning the Doctor went to the barn to feed his horse, and found that some one had entered the barn and shaved his horse's mane and tail close to the skin; and, besides, had cut our buffalo robe all in pieces; besides shaving the horse, the villains had cut his ears off. It was the most distressing looking animal you ever saw. It was indeed to be pitied. The Dr. gathered up the fragments of the buffalo robe and brought them to the house; it was a sight to behold!

We intended to have left that day, but we changed our minds and stayed over another night, and held another meeting. The house was crowded to excess that evening; at the close of the service the Doctor told how some one had shaved and cut his horse, and brought out the cut robe and held it up before the people saying: "This is the way the friends of slavery have treated me. Those who have done it are known, but I shall not hurt a hair of their heads. I hope the Lord may forgive them." The people seemed to feel very badly about it.

We left the next day for another place; the name I cannot recall now. We had better success when we went to Torringford, for here the people had just passed through a terrible mob, on account of an anti-slavery lecturer. The mob broke the windows of the church, and the lecturer had to escape for his life. We arrived here on Saturday, and put up with one of the deacons of the church. The next morning, after breakfast, he harnessed up his horse and sleigh, (for it was winter), and he and his family and I drove off to the church. Every eye was upon me. The deacon said to me: "Follow me, and sit with me in my pew." I did so, and every eye was fixed upon me, I being a colored man; and, being seated in a deacon's pew, caused quite a stir or bustle among the worshipers. There was such a commotion that the minister could hardly preach.

At the close of the service one of the other deacons came to the one that I was with, and seemed to be much excited. My friend asked him: "What is the matter, you appear to be mad?" "No," says he, "I am not mad; but grieved to think that you have taken that nigger into the pew with you; I think you had better promote your own niggers instead of strangers." My friend told him that "the pew was his; that he had paid for it, and that he had the right to have any one sit with him whom he chose; and that he did not think that it was anybody's business." When the controversy was over we went home and ate dinner.

In the afternoon we started for the church again, and after arriving there I took my seat with the deacon; it did not affect the worshipers so much this time as it did in the morning. After the meeting closed we started for home and ate our supper; and in the evening the Doctor and I intended to have the church for our lecture.

On arriving there, Oh! such a crowd met us at the door that we could hardly get in. Through perseverance we made our way to the pulpit and took our seats. Some of the men who were engaged in the mob a few months before came and took the front seats, and looked as though they could devour us. I did not know what would become of us that night.

We began our meeting. The Doctor spoke first. They did not intend to have him speak, (being a white man), for the men were desirous to hear me; they kept quiet, however, for the sake of hearing me. When the Doctor was through I took the stand, and before I had finished my talk took all the fight out of them; some of them wept like children; so you see that it changed those men's hearts towards us, for a sympathetic feeling seemed to pervade through their hearts. I made many friends for myself that night. I heard one of them say that "if my master came there after me he would fight for me as long as he had a drop of blood in him." There were no more mobs in Torringford after that.

We then started for other parts of the State, and the work of the Lord prospered in our hands. I went back to Wilbraham and lectured in the hall to a large audience; and from there I went to South Wilbraham, and spoke in the M.E. Church to a full house. Many that heard of the sufferings of the poor slave, wept like children; many turned from slavery to anti-slavery. I went from South Wilbraham to Boston, and spoke in the Spring Street Church before a large assembly. I spoke in Worcester, and many left the slavery ranks and joined the anti-slavery. I have spoken in some places in Connecticut where the people have acted as though they had never seen a colored man before; they would shake hands with me and then look at their hands to see if I had left any black on them. I met with success every where I went; I traveled all the winter of 1842 with the Doctor, and in the spring following I left him and returned to Springfield, to resume my trade again, (boot and shoe-making), and worked a few months.

During my first year with Mr. Elmore I formed an acquaintance with a young lady, Miss Emeline Minerva Platt, who was visiting one fourth of July a friend of mine, at whose home I boarded for a time. At this time I had made up my mind to settle North, and had given up all idea of ever visiting my Southern friends. As I had often seen this lady, in company with other friends, I thought it would be a good opportunity, on this occasion, to offer my hand in marriage.

Four years from my first acquaintance, in the spring of 1842, we were married. I have three daughters and one son.

VI | LIFE IN NORWICH, CONN.

*Came to Norwich—Started business—Purchase a
house—Persecutions and difficulties—Ministerial
labors—Church troubles—Formation of a new Methodist
Church—Retiring from ministerial work—Amos B.
Herring—Mary Humphreys—Sketches of life and
customs in Africa.*

I n coming to Norwich, Conn., in 1842, I took a shop on
Main Street, near where Perkins Block, now stands; here I
remained one year. The next year, 1843, I moved across Franklin
Square, in the rear of Chapman's Block, the place now occupied
by R. R. Armstrong as a fish-market; here I remained till I was
burned out. This shop contained a side-room, which was occupied by John Wells, who hired it of me, and was employed as a
boot black. On one night of the fire he was asleep in his room,
and came very near loosing his life; by breaking his door open
he was rescued from the burning flames. This shop was burned
to the ground. I then moved to a shop on Shetucket Street, and
from here to a shop in Chapman's Block, where I remained for
a number of years. I then secured a shop on Bath Street, where
I am located at the present time.

In first coming to Norwich, I established myself in business with a full line of customers. I then looked about for a tenement to live in and succeeded in finding one, through a friend, on Franklin Street, and then I returned to Massachusetts for my wife, who came in June. After living two years and-a-half on this street, I moved to a tenement on School Street, where I remained one year. The next year I had accumulated money enough to pay one-half for a frame house— only a few steps from where I then lived—before taking possession of it. Three years from this time I paid off all the mortgage on the house; then I truly felt that it was my own, since through my energy and toil, I had gained it.

In establishing myself in business, Mr. Gurdon A. Jones, a wholesale shoe dealer, patronized me by giving me his custom work. He was the first shoe dealer who gave me work, and this greatly assisted me towards my accumulations.

As the years rolled on my family began to increase so that I deemed it necessary to procure a larger house. Having made several attempts, I bought a desirable one on Oak Street. After a struggle of a few years we moved into our new home. Reader, you must not think that I obtained it without any trouble. Ah! no; it was under difficulties; I had many a heart ache: I was persecuted on every hand for getting a home. While many would be encouraged for their industry and toil, my people are subject to all sorts of abuse for buying desirable homes for their families. We were in Norwich when colored young men were not allowed to attend the High School that was kept for young men on School Street. A promising young man of color applied for admission, and was promptly rejected. It is owing to being deprived of the chance to acquire an education that many of the old inhabitants, and the young, are ignorant today.

We were waiting with anxious expectation for the day

to dawn, to enjoy all our privileges and equal rights as citizens. We have waded through many trials, and suffered every thing but death itself, in endeavoring to educate our children; many a time they have been to school with a heavy heart while trying to solve some problem or translation. Oh! how my heart went out for them; they were not easily daunted, for they were filled with enthusiastic ardor; they shrank from no obstacles. The old saying is, "the darkest hour is just before dawn."

My two daughters, Louie Amelia Smith, and Emma J.I. Smith, after completing, the former a classical and the latter an English course at the Norwich Free Academy, in Norwich, graduated from that institution, and thus qualified themselves for future usefulness. They have proved very successful as teachers in Washington, D.C. My eldest daughter, Sarah Ann Smith, a graduate from the Normal Grammar School, is living at home and making herself useful. My son, James H. Smith, follows the trade of his father.

The first commencement of my ministerial labors, after I came to Norwich, was in a Union Church on Allen Street. There were two colored denominations which worshiped in this church—the Methodists and Presbyterians; both societies had a share in this church. The agreement was that each denomination were to take their turns in leading the meetings. The Methodists were very anxious to have me preach for them, and the Presbyterians desired a pastor of their own persuasion. The upper part of the church was used for the Sabbath school, and the basement for the preaching services. The reason for this was, because the regular audience room was not finished. The stove was moved to either part of the house, to suit their convenience. Prayer and class meetings were often held during the week at private houses. The Methodists were very zealous, and generally conducted the services on the Sabbath that the Presbyterians rightfully claimed. This caused a strife among them, and then a controversy arose with reference to the two ministers.

One evening while I was preaching, a red hot stove was carried out from the upper part of the church into the street by the opposite party; when the heat had abated somewhat, they carried it into the basement. The lights were put out, leaving me in total darkness; the meeting got fairly beyond control; the seats and floor were well besmeared with oil. More lamps were procured from the neighboring houses, and I continued the services till we were completely frozen out, and were obliged to close before the usual time. The other party continued till after nine o'clock.

The two societies never became reconciled to each other, and consequently there was a split in the church. The Presbyterians stayed at their post, while the Methodists went off by themselves, and gave up all they had put in the church to the Presbyterians. To keep themselves together, they held meetings at private houses, of great spiritual power. This separation weakened the Presbyterians somewhat, and they disbanded soon after, as the Methodists formed the larger part of the congregation. Prior to this a singing school was opened, and they made a vast improvement in the singing. Thus was the beginning of my first trials in the ministry.

The Methodists, after awhile, bought a building lot in the rear of Franklin Street, of William Prentice, for which they paid him two hundred dollars. Rev. Leaven Tilman came to Norwich to aid us in organizing a Methodist Church, as it was his business to organize churches wherever they were needed. He went around to solicit funds for that purpose, and was very zealous in the work. Myself and others, with his aid, solicited funds for purchasing the ground, and for the building. After the house was completed it was dedicated to the Lord. At the dedication, Bishop Quinn, Bishop Clark, Rev. H. J. Johnson, and others, were present and conducted the services.

We opened a Sabbath school and were prospered in our good work; we formed a bible-class, and opened a singing school. The bible-class consisted of young men who had formed themselves into a club called the "Young Men's Christian Association." Every Sabbath they were found in their places, and the class was in a flourishing condition.

The church was under the supervision of our New England Conference, which supplied us with ministers. I preached for the people of this parish for twenty years. We experienced many refreshing seasons; death invaded our ranks, calling out some very faithful and efficient helpers. The Sabbath school was broken up on account of the death of its prominent leaders.

At the time of the great rebellion the young men of the church disbanded and responded readily to their country's call. Although there were many obstacles to retard the progress of the church, yet there were a few who held on and hoped for better days. I was ordained Deacon, at the New England Conference, and after being with them four years, they appointed me Local Deacon. During my whole ministry in the church, I had no regular salary; I worked at my trade to support myself and family. I was compelled, by growing infirmities to retire from my pastoral labors, feeling that the days of my active usefulness were almost over. The house of worship became so dilapidated as the years rolled on that we sold it, and it passed into other hands.

After Mr. Gurdon A. Jones' decease, the well-known firms of E. G. Bidwell, J. H. Kelley, and J. F. Cosgrove employed me for years to do their custom work, which was quite a pecuniary assistance and help to me.

During my stay in Springfield, Mass., I became acquainted with a man by the name of Amos B. Herring, a native of Africa. It seems he had been on to Springfield once before, but, not having finished his education, he had returned to complete his course at Wilbraham Academy. He was a widower with six boys, the two eldest of whom he had left in Paris, to be educated, while he had come here. His wife had been dead four years; so he left his beautifully furnished house in Monrovia in charge of a housekeeper, paying her a dollar a month—just here you will see how low wages were in Africa. He told me every thing was nearly as cheap as could be. He had not been in Springfield long before he became acquainted with a Mrs. Lucy Terret, of Washington, D.C. They married; but upon his returning to Africa his wife did not long survive. She had made a great many friends during her stay in Springfield, and when he wrote back that his wife was dead we could not but regret that she ever left us. Soon after her arrival in Monrovia she was attacked with a fever, from which she died. She was very fond of the tropical fruit which abounded, such as bananas, bread-fruit and dates, and had been cautioned about eating it before she was fully acclimated. At one time it was thought she would live through the attack, but she insisted on tasting the fruit, which she appeared to enjoy better than any thing else. A daughter by a former marriage—a sweet and attractive child—also found a grave in a foreign land.

Another friend of mine, Miss Mary Humphreys, also went to Africa as a missionary, and established a school in Monrovia. Her sole object in going was to do all the good she could in the way of enlightening her people. Soon she was smitten down with the African fever. So we see it is almost impossible for persons from this country to live in that climate. Very few survive the fever, and the fever they must have. I remember when there was so much talk about emigrating to Liberia that quite a number of my people embarked for the foreign land. Accounts afterwards showed that most of them died, if not on shipboard, soon after they reached shore.

Mr. Herring and myself often enjoyed many pleasant conversations. I used to love to hear him tell of Africa I had read so much about. He said that Monrovia was quite a thriving town then, and a great speculative mart for merchants of all nations. Many of the merchants who live there can not own lands, but can hire them. In passing the king, the white man is obliged to take off his hat. It is necessary, in presenting yourself before a chief or king, to carry a lot of presents to insure a welcome, notwithstanding they may not be of very great value; but they must be showy, such as bright colored shirts, and red cloth which is worn to adorn the breast pocket. Only a few of the Africans are able to wear stripes of red cloth. Some are clad entirely in shirts made of leather, which they skillfully prepare. I was quite amused at his account of a chief who consumed daily a sheep and the milk of seven cows.

The king partook of a kind of macaroni, prepared from wheat, with a rich seasoning of butter; while the natives ate apples pounded up and simmered down, in the place of real butter, which they considered very good. The natives burnt a kind of brush to keep the panthers and hyenas away, which abounded in large numbers.

In speaking of Africa, I would say that slavery still exists there. Slave ships are traveling to and fro from Africa to many of our foreign ports laden with slaves. We look forward to the day when Africa shall be free, and my people shall have that liberty that rightfully belongs to them. Many missionaries have gone out there to enlighten and teach the natives the "Good Way;" but after awhile we find most of them more interested in the gold and silver than in the civilization of the people.

In referring to the chief who consumed a sheep every day, you must not think this species were as large as the American sheep. These animals were not fattened like the sheep among us. They were very lean, and scarcely any fat on their ribs. They resided in the dense forests, and sought their own food, and subsisted on all kinds of nuts, tropical fruits, or anything they could find to eat. They inhabited the interior of Western Africa, and other parts of the country. The cows, also, for the want of care and green pasture fields to feed in, were not as large in size as those in America; and, for this reason, they gave a small supply of milk daily. It required a supply of milk from seven cows in order to obtain milk enough for the chief.

VII THE WAR OF THE REBELLION

Desire to return to Virginia—Opening of the War—
Disdain of the aid of colored men—Defeat—Progress of
the War—Employing colored men—Emancipation
Proclamation—Celebration—Patriotism of Colored
Soldiers—Bravery at Port Hudson—Close of the War—
Death of Lincoln—A tribute to Senator Sumner—
Passage of the Civil Rights Bill—Our Standard Bearers.

For many years, while slavery existed, I have never ceased to pray that God, in his all wise providence would bring it to pass that I might return to the land that gave me birth, and see my former friends. As the signs of the times looked dark and doubtful, I began to think I should never realize such a blessing; but time passed on, and with it the rebellion increased in strength, war rumors were afloat, and the very air seemed to bespeak war. God gave us war signs which spoke of the dissolution of the Union. Some said in case of a war between the North and South, that it would result in the liberation of the slave. I said it would be too good a blessing to be true, not dreaming that such a course would lead to it; not knowing which way the scales would turn. We all know the immediate cause of the rebellion. The North and South were at length arrayed against each other in two great political parties on the question of slavery. The Northern party triumphed, and though no unlawful act was charged against it, and no simulated claim or assumption offered that it had not succeeded in a lawful and constitutional way, the defeated Southern party refused to accept the decision of the ballot box, and rushing into open revolt proceeded to organize a government of its own. Not being satisfied in what they already possessed they craved for more territory, and fired on Fort Sumpter for that purpose in the spring of 1861, little dreaming that they themselves were destroying their beloved institution.

The first sound of the cannon that saluted the ears of Major Anderson, and his starving garrison, was the death knell of slavery. The heart of the nation beat in unison; every telegraph wire vibrated with the news, "Sumpter has fallen." The news spread like the flash of lightning through the country; it united the people and aroused the nation to a sense of its duty; the proud sons of America responded as one to the call of their country. It was then this war began in which we have all had to take our part. When President Lincoln called for men to defend the country, the call was for white men. Our martyred President, proud in the strength of his high position said, "the Union must be saved with slavery, if it can, without it, if it must." Did he forget that at the great wheel of state there was a guiding hand, stronger and mightier, and more just than his. Truly, "God moves in a mysterious way, His wonders to perform."

At the beginning of the war, few anticipated the great and important changes so soon to be wrought by it. To the observing eye, the hand of God has been seen in the war; seen in the overthrow of the proud, and uplifting of the lowly; seen in the fall of the taskmaster and the emancipation of the slave. Many fought for the liberation of the colored man, although they hated him. How well do I remember the time when our Northern army undertook to go into battle at Bull Run. The Northerners, corrupted by unexampled prosperity, and forgetful of the traditions of their forefathers, the vital and animating principles underlying the very foundation of this government, severed their course from the cause of liberty and every hope by which the black man might take courage, proclaiming it to be the white man's war exclusively. The Northerners, eager for glory and greedy for honor in that eventful hour disdained the proffered service of the colored man, and would not even permit him to drive a wagon in train of their army; and even more, would not allow him to wear the cast-off clothing of their soldiers for fear the imperial blue of this great republic would be dishonored by them, and perverted from a sacred purpose.

Under such circumstances, the Northern troops, filled with pride and haughtiness, promptly responding to the call, "On to Richmond," moved in military order to plant their standard on the walls of Richmond. Not a military instrument of music, or drum cheered the march; the deep silence broken only by the muffled tread of the advancing host, or the heavy rumbling of the artillery carriages. On their march they were confronted at Bull Run by an army animated by a sterner and more determined will. The rising sun of the ever memorable 21st of July, 1891, beheld the Union troops in "war's bright and stern array;" their polished arms shone in the morning's light, and their silken banners glittering in the sun. The long line of bayonets flashing in the sunbeams, extended rows of army wagons with their white tops, winding columns of cavalry, the dark looking ambulances, all combined to form a scene of thrilling interest, and presented a magnificent spectacle.

But the parting rays of that same sun looked down on defeated, routed and disgraced men; their bright arms thrown away, and their silken banners were taken by the exulting Rebels as trophies of war, or trailed in the dust. Then, forgetful of all their proud boastings, our Northern troops made a hasty retreat towards Washington. The panic was disgraceful in the extreme; for miles the road was black with men running in all directions. Hosts of Federal troops, some separated from their regiments, were fleeing along the road and through the fields, all mingled in one disorderly route. Horses galloped at random, riderless from the battle-field, many of them in the agonies of death swelling the wild commotion. Then the heavy artillery, such as was not destroyed, came thundering along, overturning and smashing every thing in its passage. Hacks conveying spectators from the battle-field were completely smashed, leaving the occupants to the mercy of the way. Sutler's teams, carriages and army wagons blockaded the passage way, and fell against each other amidst the dense cloud of dust. Men lying seriously wounded along the banks entreated, with raised hands, those on horse-back to lift them further back, so they might not be trod on.

The Northern troops, in this celebrated race of twenty-five miles, with forty thousand entries, was made without stopping; for the goal was Washington, and the prize safety. Though taxed to their utmost, it is sorrowful to reflect that all this haste and endurance were needlessly expanded. We have the facts in history that the Southerners did not pursue the Union army, and they did not find out the mistake till after the flight. This lesson was terrible to the North, but it was not sufficient to teach them to do justice to the downtrodden of my people; and, still relying on their superior numbers and almost boundless resources, the government called for three hundred thousand more men.

It was at this time that the whole North, humbled by defeat, and eager to revenge the Rebels, sprang to arms. Soon there was a gathering of the clans from the rivers to the lakes, and from ocean to ocean. Geo. B. McClellan, of the West, led a mighty host towards Richmond, and by a new route. The earth shook beneath the tread of his army, and the ocean was filled with his iron-clad war ships. Being chained down by fate in the pestilential swamps of the Chickahominy, daring not to strike, and unwilling to retreat, he permitted the golden moments to pass until his army was decimated by disease. The South then took fresh courage, and gathered from her broad dominions her best and bravest sons and threw them, with irresistible force, upon his defeated army. Indignant and morose, our army sought safety beneath the guns of the fleet, otherwise every one of them would have been annihilated.

It was under these circumstances of gloom and despondency that our beloved martyr President lifted himself to the height of his great duties; issued the immortal proclamation of emancipation, proclaiming liberty to the oppressed millions made in the image of God; severing the chains from the limbs of hundreds of thousands. Their shouts of joy for new-born liberty had rung over distant hills, and through wooded dales.

I was then keeping shop in Chapman's Block, on Franklin Square, when the proclamation of freedom was proclaimed; it sent a thrill of joy through every avenue of my soul. I exclaimed, "Glory to God, peace on earth, and good will to men," for the year of jubilee has come! His glorious Proclamation of Emancipation will stamp the first of January,

1863, as the day of days; the great day of jubilee to millions. When that battle cry resounded throughout the land, o'er river and plains, o'er mountains and glens, even then the government could not entirely emancipate itself from the hateful spirit of caste. Still awed by the tradition of the past, it had not the courage to say to the freedmen: "We want you to fight in defence of the life of the nation;" but they said: "We want you as laborers, and for your better organization and control we will enroll you in companies, and form you into a regiment, and for your protection, we will arm you."

It was by this sneaking, back-door arrangement, that they were smuggled surreptitiously into the service of our country. It was plainly seen that the American people, at first, were unwilling that the colored man should go into the battle—it was "the white man's war, and negroes had nothing to do with it." When the Governor of the State of Ohio was asked if he would accept of a colored company, he replied that they "didn't want negroes,"—and for the love to their country went to Massachusetts and enlisted, with the promise of the pitiful sum of seven dollars a month. And not until the Massachusetts Governor received the colored man as a soldier did the governors of the other Northern States think they could condescend to give the negro a musket and a suit of blue. These are facts that can not truthfully be denied. It was not the intention of the government at the beginning of the war to free the slaves, but they soon learned that men of color were made for a nobler purpose than to be "drawers of water and hewers of wood."

As a war necessity, the Americans bestirred themselves for their protection; they were driven to take measures that neither God, justice nor humanity could induce them to adopt, knowing that the Rebels armed the slaves to fight against them, for they saw that they were likely to be defeated. It has been said that colored men will not fight for liberty, but will run at the first fire. They questioned their loyalty, and distrusted their fighting qualities. When we think of the Bull Run race, we have nothing to say about running. Let me direct your attention to that brave fifty-fourth Massachusetts colored regiment, who marched in the line of battle when more than one-third of their number had fallen, their color-bearer lying in the cold embrace of death, when a Mr. Wall, of Oberlin, grasped the flag, mounted the parapet and waved over the conquered enemy the stars and stripes. If that is not bravery, I ask what is? Is it running? We find them running to replace the flag of our country in the very capital of the Rebels, and we as a nation need not be ashamed of this kind of running.

I commend the daring and noble deeds of our soldiers, and hand them down to posterity as worthy of imitation, and that they have won for themselves a proud position on the pages of American history. Thanks be to God the colored men, as soldiers, have shown to the world their true patriotism in their valor and courage, and displayed as dauntless bravery as ever illuminated a battle field. Thousands have fought and died. They met death calmly, bravely defending the cause that we revere. The world has looked on with admiration and wonder at the boldness and daring of their victorious host, for they have contributed largely towards some of its splendid victories. They have come forward by thousands, and rallied around the so called "banner of the free," hoping that by preserving it from the hands of the enemy to make our dear beloved country free—what she has so long been called in song and story: "The land of the free and the home of the brave,"—after two hundred years or more of oppression and injustice, and having not only their rights as citizens, but their manhood ignored; and,

besides, a thousand other wrongs calculated to kill the patriotism in any other than a black man.

An incident of bravery of the colored troops at Port
Hudson, I am about to relate, sends a thrill through every
avenue of my soul. I wish it could be burned into our hearts
with words of fire, so that no tongue would henceforth dare
to utter or repeat the old slander that "black men will not
fight for freedom." Let the vaunted Anglo-Saxon stand back
abashed before this sublime exhibition.

In 1863 the Fifty Second Regiment Massachusetts Colored Volunteers were ordered to charge the enemy's works,
and did it magnificently. Just before they reached the forts they
came to a ditch thirty feet wide and ten feet deep, full of water,
which was absolutely impassable; they were ordered forward
again; they could only do and die, yet on, right on they went
to the hopeless charge; into the storm of grape and musket
balls; on, with no chance of doing any thing but to die like
brave men; on, where their white officers dare not to lead, till
nearly half their number were dead or dying. Five times more
they charged up to this bayou, when they were withdrawn.

When I think of these torn and bleeding veterans as
they wended their way to the hospital, it seems too horrible
to relate. Nevertheless it is so, for I have the facts. I can
hardly speak of it but with many tears. Bless God that they
have shown themselves worthy to be free, and entitled to all
the inalienable rights, among which are "life, liberty, and the
pursuit of happiness;" having won the rights for all their
posterity, without having them infringed upon, for they are
blood-bought rights. Can a people into whose hands arms
have been placed, and who have been drilled in the art and
science of war, become again slaves? And can this nation,
that has advanced so rapidly in the cause of freedom, go
backwards so much as to re-enslave a people that have

assisted in fighting its battles? Forbid it, justice! forbid it, humanity! forbid it, ye spirits of our fathers, still hovering over us! forbid it, our Country! forbid it, Heaven!

In the spring of 1865 the war closed; then the lovers of the Union, and freedom, were giving thanks to God for recent victories they had gained, and rejoiced that right and justice had triumphed over wrong. City after city fell, until Richmond itself was surrendered to a band of colored warriors.

There are times when the human heart is so overwhelmed with joy and gratitude, with thanksgiving and praise, that words seem meaningless, and language fails to convey the deep emotion felt. Words were inadequate to convey the joy unspeakable, and almost full of glory, that the lovers of the Union felt at that hour of triumph. Great were the rejoicings over the fall of Richmond; beautiful were the displays made in all the places, far and near. Flags were thrown out to the breeze, bells resounded, bonfires, illuminations; the rocket's red glare, and the cannon boomed forth its peals of thunder. The innumerable lights which flashed forth their brilliancy threw into magnificent relief the gorgeous decorations of the buildings. Crowds of human beings of all sexes, nationalities and colors assembled in the streets; they were wild with excitement; they were crazy with joy; enthusiasm cannot describe it. Men hugged each other, struck one another, yelled and screamed like wild men.

Peace, with its snowy wings, seemed to be hovering in the air, ready to shed its blessings on the distracted and blood-drenched country. Richmond, for four long years of blood and tears, of fire and sword, was at last convulsed in its last death-throe. Events of magnitude crowded upon us in such rapidity that before we could duly digest the one, another of more startling importance rushed in and pushed it aside. Before we had half thought out the evacuation of

Richmond, then came the sudden news of the surrender of Gen. Lee, and the Confederate army of Virginia.

But ah! our day of rejoicing had scarcely passed when the same wires that brought the tidings of the surrender of Lee, brought the sad intelligence that our beloved President was dead—fallen by the hand of an assassin! Oh, what a shock to the American people. Our rejoicing was turned into mourning: the whole country was draped in mourning; every eye was dimmed with tears. Pen can not begin to describe the sadness; deeply the people felt the loss of one whom they loved as a father. The American Nation has lost a pure patriot; humanity a tried friend; freedom a great champion. He was stricken down at the time when his great wisdom was so much needed in bringing his distracted and blood-drenched country into the harbor of returning peace and prosperity. His course, from the time of inauguration, had been marked with wisdom and justice; his manner had been unfaltering; his feelings could be touched by all classes of the nation, from the highest to the lowest—an instrument in the hands of God in avenging and redressing the wrongs of years, and the emancipator of my heretofore enslaved brethren of the South. None were afraid to approach his Excellency, and justice was always meted out, as the circumstances of the case required. It was my desire that he might have witnessed the end of the beginning; but, as Moses, he viewed, but was not permitted by Divine Providence to reach the end of the beginning, which began to loom up with such splendor. The position he placed us in, as a people, causes us to feel as did the children of Israel when they passed through the Red Sea, and were freed from the hand of Pharaoh and his pursuing host. ABRAHAM LINCOLN has gone but a step before us, but ever memorable will be his name in the hearts of the loyal millions.

In Memoriam

We also pay tribute to the late Senator Summer, that in his death, we, and the friends of freedom everywhere have lost a sincere and earnest friend, an able and untiring philanthropist and statesman; the principle of freedom he strove so earnestly to inculcate into the minds of all, irrespective of complexion. It was his last and most deeply cherished wish to lift up the colored race to the plane of perfect equality. "See to the Civil Rights Bill, don't let it fail," were among his last utterances to his colleague, who stood beside the dying Senator. Probably at no period of his life did he more forcibly illustrate his perseverance, his energy, his zeal and eloquence than in the many efforts he made to pass this bill. That bill was the great work which was to crown his labors. We never can express the sentiments of gratitude which his name awakens in the breast of every colored American. In defending the rights of my people by the most generous sentiments of his aspiring nature, by his sincere love of justice, he has acquired an immortal title to all their descendants. The Civil Rights Bill, passed April 9th, 1866.

Our Standard Bearers

Thomas Garrett, James and Lucretia Mott, Francis Jackson, Wendell Phillips, William Lloyd Garrison, Henry C. Wright, Owen Lovejoy, Lydia Maria Childs, Abby Kelly Foster, the Phelpses, Samuel Budgett, and many others, by their pen and voice poured floods of light upon the minds and hearts of the public, through evil as well as through good report, until they have created unto God, and developed that moral and religious influence which has always accomplished that to which they consecrated themselves, and for which they strove with a devotion as constant as truth, and with an industry and zeal as unwavering as justice, and with a fidelity as pure as their cause was patriotic and sacred. Let them, and many others shine as stars, for they were as beacon lights for freedom. They spoke when speech cost something; their greeting was the violence of the mob, and their baptism fire and blood. They did not "count their lives dear unto themselves." The sufferings and death of Torrey Lovejoy and John Brown, has sent a thrill through the hearts of the nation, for they possessed a self-sacrificing spirit. Let their names be written as with a diamond; let the historian stamp them with letters of fire upon tablets of gold; let the poet sing them in sweet strains; let the scholar, with the graces of literature, embalm them; let the great of humanity enshrine them. Their deeds can never be effaced, but will exist as an imperishable memento, engraven on the hearts of the people.

VIII | AFTER THE WAR

*Fear of capture—A visit to Heathsville—Father
Christmas, and a children's festival—Preaching at
Washington—My first visit to my old home—Joy and
rejoicing—Meeting my old mistress—My old cabin
home—The old spring—Change of situations—The old
doctor—Improvement in the condition of the colored
people—Buying homes—Industry.*

After the Fugitive Slave Law was passed, terror struck the hearts of those who had escaped to the free States, as no earthly power could prevent them from being returned to their masters. Very many were taken back. For my part, I was very much frightened, and was continually haunted by dreams which were so vivid as to appear really true. One night I dreamt my master had come for me, and, as he proved property, I was delivered up to him by the United States Marshal. In the morning I told the dream to my wife. She said she "believed it would come true," and was very much worried.

I went down to my shop, and, in the course of the morning, while looking out of my window I noticed a number of persons who had just come in on the train, and among them I was sure I saw my master. You may rest assured I was pretty well frightened out of my wits. What to do I did not know. This man did certainly walk like him, had whiskers like him; in fact his whole general appearance resembled his so much that I was sure that he had been put on my track. I peeped out at him as he passed my door and saw him go up the steps leading to the office of the U.S. Marshal, then I was sure he had come for me. I could do no more work that day.

As my friends came in I told them of what I had seen, my fears, etc.; and they assured me they would be on the look-out and see if such a man was in town, find out his errand, etc. Accordingly one of them who was a town crier, Dunton by name, went to the hotels and searched the registers to see if a man by the name of Lackey was registered there. At night he reported that no such name could be found. My friends declared that I should not leave this town. One even went so far as to go to the U.S. Marshal and ask if "any one should come, looking for me, what he would do; would he give me up?" He replied: "No, he'd resign his position first." Another bought a revolver, and told me that "if they had me up that, by some means, he would manage it so as to get it into my hands that I might in some way defend myself." I had determined never to be taken back alive. Death was preferable to slavery, now that I had tasted the sweets of liberty. As it was, dreams of this kind ceased to trouble me, and the effects and fear wore off.

It was not till after the Emancipation Proclamation, that a man who is living in Norwich today, told me that after I left the South, and had settled here, he went to Heathsville, to the very place where I used to live, saw my master, who asked him whether, in his travels North, he had ever come across a man who was lame, shoemaker by trade; that he would give him two hundred dollars, cash, for any information which would lead to his discovery. He returned home, said nothing whatever to me, for fear I would be alarmed, sell out and leave the place; said nothing to any one about it till after January 1st, 1863, when freedom was proclaimed throughout the land.

During one of my visits to Heathsville, on which I always carried a large stock of clothing, shoes, etc., I formed a plan for some amusement among the young people. On Sunday it was announced that on a certain evening during the week there would be a Christmas tree. All were invited to come; accordingly when the time arrived, the church was packed; many came from miles away. I selected a young man who I intended should represent Father Christmas, as he is called there. I put on him a long swallow tail coat, the ends of which almost touched the floor, then he was filled out so as to be very large; he had on an extremely sharp pointed collar, which extended far out from his face, which was hidden behind a mask. I opened with an address, and at a given signal, Father Christmas made his first appearance. Many of the children, even some of the old people were frightened nearly out of their wits; one child ran forward, crying to his Uncle John to save him; some fell over each other to get out of the way. Well, I laughed till I could laugh no longer, and finally I was obliged to dispense with Father Christmas before anything like order could be obtained. Then the different articles were distributed, and if you could have heard the many prayers that went up from thankful hearts for the gifts received, no one would tire of this good work. General satisfaction reigned, and after a hymn of thanksgiving they dispersed to their homes.

January, 1867, I was called to visit Washington, to see

about a school for my daughter. While there I was invited by
the pastor of Israel Church to preach on the Sabbath. At the
close of the service many of my former friends came forward to greet me, and informed me of the old plantation
where my brother and two sisters still resided. I immediately
wrote to my brother to let him know that I was still alive,
and that I should visit Heathsville at such a time, and asked
him if "he thought there would be any danger in coming."
He informed me that "there was no danger, for Virginia was
free." When he received the letter it seemed as from one
risen from the dead. My sister took the letter and went
round amongst her friends wild with joy.

A few weeks after this I made preparations to start on
my long-premeditated journey, in the middle of June, 1867.
I went by way of Washington. As I was proceeding down the
old Potomac River her red banks looked natural to me, so
much so that I could hardly suppress the feeling of joy
which arose in my heart. That night the boat stopped about
forty miles from Heathsville. The next morning, about light,
I went ashore, as I was very anxious to tread once more on
the old Virginia soil. Very soon the bell rang for the boat to
start; I hastened on board again. By this time she had got
underway, and I reached Cone Wharf at six o'clock—the
very spot from where I started thirty years before. It seemed
to me more like a dream than a reality. No one can imagine
how I felt; I could not believe that it was possible that I was
going home to tread on free soil. I asked myself the question: "Can it be possible that Virginia is free?" I looked
ashore before the boat reached the landing, and saw those
old ex-slave-holders standing on the dock, which sent a
thrill all over me. But soon the boat rounded up to the
dock, and as soon as the gang-plank was put out there were
some white young men who came aboard and stepped up

to the bar and began drinking. A colored man, also, went up to get something to drink. There was a row that commenced with the white men and the colored man, and came very near ending in a fight. Here I saw the old spirit of slavery exhibited by the whites. This somewhat increased my fears; but quiet was soon restored, and I stepped ashore almost on the same spot where I was thirty years before.

Things looked changed somewhat since I left, but after awhile I came to myself and found that I was really home again, unmolested where I was once a slave, and my joy knew no bounds. I was soon discovered by some of my friends, and we congratulated one another like old friends, for I seemed to them like one risen from the grave. I felt as though I wanted to get down and kiss the free ground upon which I stood. I could hardly restrain my feelings, for it was a new day with me. This visit was fraught with many sad reminiscences of the past.

After looking about and seeing the many changes that had been wrought in thirty years, I was taken by my friends and conveyed to my brother's house. One my way, I came to the old mill, gray with age, where I used to work. In the mill was a little room partitioned off where I had in former days done shoe-making. We stopped, and I went into the little room and saw where my bench used to stand, and the old, quaint fireplace where I used to make my fire. While I was there I remembered the joys and sorrows that I had passed through during the time I occupied that room. I then went to look for the old spring where I used to get water; I found it and knelt down by the side of it and drank therefrom. No language could express my feelings while I knelt over that spring. I then arose and continued my journey till I came to a cross-path, which I traveled in my former day. I asked the driver if "he would halt and let me get out of the wagon," and told him that "he could drive around and I would go across." As I viewed the place, old scenes seemed so natural to me that I could not help praising God in the highest for bringing me back to the place of my birth. I waited a few minutes, and then proceeded on. We then came to the old Heathsville spring, here I got out also and stooped to drink. We then came to the village of Heathsville, and as soon as I entered it, I was recognized by old friends who knew me in former days. I alighted from the wagon and we clasped each other, and a full tide of joy rushed over our souls. Here I found my brother's wife, he having been sold years before. After looking around at the different places where I had lived, and the different shops where I had worked. I started for my brother's house, located about two miles out of the village of Heathsville. When I was within half-a-mile of his house, I meet my brother coming out of the house of a friend, and as soon as I saw him I knew him, although I had not seem him for years.

Dear reader, you should have been there in order to have realized the scene of our meeting. We got hold of each other and put our arms around each other's neck without speaking for some minutes; the silence was broken, and I exclaimed: "Dear brother, is it possible that we are standing on Virginia's free soil, and we are free?" My brother replied, "yes, dear brother, and you too have been living in the 'land of the free and the home of the brave.'" We wept and rejoiced, and praised God for his goodness in bringing us together once more on free soil. For a short time all was excitement and confusion. When it had subsided we started for the house, where I met my eldest sister. She pressed eagerly forward to greet me, and we seemed to each other as one risen from the dead. We, too, fell on each other's neck and clasped each other and wept. News spread like-fire that Lindsey Payne (for that was my name before I escaped from slavery,) had returned home again. Many of my old friends who once knew me, came flocking in to see me. My listeners were never weary, as I related to them the history of my life at the North, and described the varied scenes through which I had passed. My joy and excitement rose to such a height, that I scarcely knew whether I was in the body or out.

In the afternoon I went down to the "great house," so-called in the days of slavery, where Mrs. Sarah Winsted lived, who was formerly my mistress. She was the second wife of my former master, Mr. Langsdon. She survived him, and afterwards married a Mr. Winsted, who died before her. When I got within two hundred yards of the house she saw me coming, and knew me. It being warm weather she threw on her sun bonnet and came to meet me, and was so glad that she wept and grasped my hand for a minute before either spoke. At last she broke the silence by saying "Oh! Lindsey, is this you?" I replied: "This is me, what there is left of me." Says Mrs. Winsted: "Let us go to the house." Mrs. Winsted then introduced me to her daughter, who had been born since I left, and then set the table and would have me take dinner with her. Although I had ate dinner, I accepted her cordial invitation as an appreciation of her kindness.

After dinner she told me "to relate to her the narrative of my escape from slavery; how I got away, and how the Yankees had treated me since I had been up amongst them?" I set my chair back, and told her the whole story of my escape. When I told her how frightened I was by seeing the cars, and thought the engine was the devil coming after me, she really did shake with laughter. I also informed her of our sail up the Chesapeake Bay in a small boat, and how we were overtaken by the storm of wind and came very near being lost, but we reached the land of freedom in safety; that the Northern people had treated me comparatively well; and that I had bought me a comfortable home. She seemed to be very much pleased with my recital. I gave her a nice pair of shoes, for which she was very thankful.

While on this visit I saw a great many places of my childhood among them were Hog Point, where I spent many of my boyhood days; and, also, the very spot where I was made lame. I saw the old oak tree that stood near my mother's cabin home, which I have mentioned in the first part of this work, on a limb of which Mr. Haney hung one of his slaves, and whipped him till the ground beneath him was stained with his blood. I tried to find the same limb, but although the tree appeared to be in perfect health and strength, that limb seemed to have withered and dropped off. While I was meditating under this tree, many scenes of my boyhood came vividly to my recollection. I then searched for my mother's cabin home, but no humble cabin, like the one in my memory, met my eye; it had given place to a dense pine forest. The logs of the cabin had either been burned or rotted with the dust of the earth. All was desolate in the extreme. I called, but there was no response; no voice of a kind mother greeted my ear; no welcome of the eleven brothers and sisters greeted my approach; all was speechless as the grave. Nothing occupied that sacred spot but the reptile and the owl. As I gazed and thought, I became faint and sorrowful. I turned from here in pursuit of the spring from which I had carried so many buckets of water. After much search and labor, crawling through the bushes and fallen trees, I found the old spring and drank therefrom. The old gum tree that was near this spring in my childhood days, I found there still, being bent with age; its branches hung over this spring. It was once noted for its healing properties, the berries of which were used for medicinal purposes.

MY OLD CABIN HOME.—*Page 98.*

These three springs that I have mentioned, have served to quench the thirst of many a weary soldier as he stooped to drink, at the time of the great rebellion. I knelt, and offered my heart in prayer and thanksgiving to "God, who doeth all things well." I thought how often my brothers and sisters with myself, came to and from that spring; but now we were separated, nearly all of us, never more to meet, till we meet in that heavenly land where father, mother and children shall never part, "where the wicked cease from troubling, and the weary are at rest." From there, with a heavy heart, I went in search of our neighbors; they, too, like the cabin, were gone; they had been committed to the dust, and their spirits had returned to "God, who gave them." Their houses were occupied by others; with a sad heart I retracted my steps to the home of Mrs. Winsted, and then to my brother's.

I spent three or four weeks in Heathsville, and while I was on this visit I went a second time to see Mrs. Winsted, and found her in the garden, in the hot sun, hoeing. Said I, "is it possible that you can work out in the hot sun?" She replied, "Lindsey, we can do a great many things when we are obliged to, that we once thought we could not do." I saw the changes that freedom had wrought, and I thought, "how people can accommodate themselves to circumstances." When we were on the plantation together she would not allow herself even to walk out doors in the hottest part of the day, without a servant to hold an umbrella over her.

Many a man who was very rich, has been reduced to beggary. Many of those negro traders, who used to buy up a large number of slaves and carry them down to the lower States and sell them, have become so poor that they have not clothes to hide their nakedness. They go around among the freedmen and beg for something to eat. I know a man who was once very rich, worth about half-a-million, who has since been reduced to such poverty that he has been obliged to hire himself out under the United States service to work on a mud machine, as a common day laborer, and is not allowed to go and see his family but once in three months, he being in Norfolk and his family in Baltimore. Others, who were rich, are even worse off than he. This description does not include all the slaveholders, for those who were kind and humane towards their slaves are far better off in circumstances than the others. The slaves, as a general thing, did not leave them in the time of the war, but stayed with them to protect their property, while their masters were on the battle field. Those who brutalized their victims seem to be marked by the vengeance of the Almighty; they are wasting away like the early dew, for many have nowhere to lay their heads, except among those whom they have abused.

The colored people, unlike all other nations on the face of the earth, are ready to fulfill that passage of Scripture: "Therefore, if thine enemy hunger, feed him; if he thirst, give him drink; for in so doing thou shalt heap coals of fire on his head." Many of them, when bleeding from the effects of the knotted whips applied by their cruel task masters, could have risen and made the land knee deep with the blood of their oppressors, and thus avenged themselves of the host of cruel wrongs which they have suffered; but, instead of raising an insurrection, they calmly left the plantations without injuring a hair of the heads of their masters, and went on the Union side; and not till the United States put arms into their hands, and bade them go forward in the defence of their country, did they attempt to show any signs of revenge.

During my first visit I noticed that very many of the houses looked very ancient and dilapidated. The old slave pens, and the whipping posts, stood just as they were when

I left. The fertile soil which once brought forth in abundance, and the cotton and corn, presented an unbroken
scene of barrenness and desolation. The place was almost
depopulated—plantations forsaken.

The South has been subjected to a fearful waste of pop-
ulation. Thousands of the colored people during the war,
and many thousands of whites also left, to say nothing of
those who have been killed. I only found one brother and
two sisters living. Since that time my eldest sister has died,
leaving four or five children, three of whom had been torn
from her, and sold into slavery, and she never heard from
them again. She was a great sufferer, owing to the want of
proper care, and sorrow reigned in her inmost soul. Finally
the Angel of Death came and severed her from her sufferings. Her husband survives her, as I write, "The fountains of
bitter sorrow are stirred by the healing branch that God can
cast." As soon as I struck the Virginia wharf, the words of the
aged colored doctor came vividly to my mind, who told me
my future destiny: "that in the course of time I would return
to my native land." Sure enough I had returned after thirty
years' absence.

A day or two after I had made my escape from slavery,
Thomas Langsdon, supposing that the old doctor was acces-
sory to my running away, fell on the man and beat him in a
brutal manner, most shocking to behold. The doctor never
recovered from his injuries; being a free man he did not have
any one to intercede for him. After I had been home a few
days, I inquired after the doctor, and found, to my great
sorrow, that he had gone to his long home, where no foe
nor hostile bands will ever enter its peaceful inclosure. In my
repeated visits to Heathsville, I observed but little improvement since the great rebellion; there have been but few
houses built for the last thirty years. The condition of the

colored people is improving very fast, for many of them are buying lands and building, and thus preparing homes for themselves. Their condition is much better than those who once owned them. The old ex-slave holders are dying off very fast. As they have no one to cultivate their large plantations, and can not do it themselves, they are obliged to divide them up and sell them to the freedmen, as they are growing over with dense forests.* I think that eventually, Virginia will be in as flourishing a condition as any section of the United States.

The Northern people are beginning to emigrate there. The steam whistle from the factory and sawmill, which serve for the employment of many, is beginning to be heard morning, noon, and night. Things begin to wear a Northern aspect considerably. The log-cabin begins to disappear in some places, giving way to houses of modern construction. The broad long handle Southern hoe is giving place to a more modern make. This improvement is more or less seen, except among the class that bought and sold human flesh, and obtained their living from the bones and sinews of others. But how have the ex-slave holders—that is including all of them in the South—treated the freed people since the great rebellion of 1861? The colored people of the South have suffered every thing, even death itself. Some were violently beaten, or rudely scourged; many were deliberately shot down in open day, on the public streets; others were way-laid and cruelly butchered, and some, God only knows the fate they have suffered. There has been an awful destruction of human life. The streets have been drenched with their blood, for it has flown freely. Many worthy and willing

---

*These pine trees had grown up from the larger trees, (saplings as they are called,) and reminded me of past days, when we slaves had to fell them for fire-wood for our masters. The woodlands were owned by them, and nothing could induce them to buy fuel to burn as long as they had slaves to labor in felling trees.

hands were left without employment, while others worked for a mere pittance to get their living, while still others toiled on as formerly, without any agreement or probability of due return. When the civil rights bill was passed, April 9th, 1866, the condition of the colored people was ameliorated in many instances.

During the rebellion some were driven from their cabins during the absence of their owners, who were on the battle field. The cabins, many of them, were stripped of all their contents, leaving the occupants nothing. Oh! how many have suffered malice and revenge, the bitter wrath and vengeance of those who justly shared the disappointments and misfortunes attending the overthrow of slavery and rebellion.

My brother is doing well, and has bought himself a nice farm, from which he raises crops every year. He is a Baptist preacher; and, besides presiding over his own church, he has the oversight of the Lancaster Baptist Church, in Lancaster County; thus supplying two churches, the Northumberland, and the Lancaster churches. My younger sister, who resides in Wycomco, in Northumberland County, Va., has four or five children; and, through her and her husband's industry have procured a small farm, from which they have obtained principally the support of their family.

During my repeated visits to Heathsville I have carried boxes of clothing and a large truck closely packed, for the benefit of the freedmen and their families. The little sacks and other children's clothes were presented to mothers whose little children stood in great need of them, and were very thankfully received. "God bless the friends of the North," was the hearty exclamation of many. I found the colored people industriously employed in doing something, and thus they seemed contented and happy.

In December, 1879, during my visit, I went down to

Fairfield, some five or six miles from Heathsville, where I had learned my trade, and found the old place much dilapidated. The fields from which were raised corn and wheat were all grown over with thick forests. The "great house" had been burned to the ground. Mrs. Winsted had passed from time into eternity to try the realities of the other world. The old shop that I used to work in had been torn down, and desolation seemed to mark the place. The foot of the war horse had been there. I tender my thanks to the kind friends of Norwich for their generous gifts.

IX | CONCLUSION

*The Fifteenth Amendment Celebration—The parade—
Address—Collation—Charles L. Remond—Closing
words.*

From 1867 to 1869, great changes were taking place in
the government. Amendments to the Consitution were
being made; among them was the fifteenth amendment.
When that was passed, the colored Americans of Norwich
called a meeting and passed a resolution proposing to celebrate that great event. In May, 1870, we appointed a committee to arrange for the same. I was appointed chairman of
that committee. A motion was made to extend a call to the
Hon. Charles L. Remond, of Boston, to deliver the oration.
The motion was unanimously passed to that effect.

The Fifteenth Amendment Celebration took place on
June 16th, 1870. At early dawn the booming of the cannon
was heard from some distant hill, that aroused the participants
to the more arduous duties of the day. The din and smoke
reminded one of the war, where our veterans fought so cred-
itably. The first part of the morning the weather did not look
very favorable for us. There was a misty appearance in the air,

but as it advanced towards ten o'clock that hazy look wore off, and the half-veiled sun shone in all its splendor. On that eventful morning the committee of arrangements labored faithfully to make the affair a success, for it was a scene of bustling activity. Flags that bore the national colors, and banners bearing mottoes appropriate for the occasion were waving in the breeze. Every effort was made by some to make it a failure, but their plans were frustrated by our eminent citizens. When undertaking a good project for our fellow-men, we are often defeated by our enemies. In this we almost lost our balance, which we soon regained in our full strength, and we came off victorious, to the astonishment of our opposers.

The generous contributions of the citizens, by way of provisions and money for the celebration, evinced their appreciation of our efforts; the arrangement reflected great credit upon those who had it in charge. The procession formed on Franklin Square, headed by the Norwich Brass and String Bands, proceeded from the Square up Washington Street, down Broadway, up Franklin Street: thence to Rockwell's Grove, where a platform was erected, upon which sat the speaker of the day, and a few of our leading citizens. One feature of the procession that attracted much attention, was a tastefully decorated car, drawn by two horses, filled with young ladies dressed in white, bearing aloft the banner of beauty and glory. The selectmen, common council, clergy, and other citizens participated in the celebration, and helped to swell the number.

A goodly number stood beneath the trees in the shady grove, and fanned by the gentle breeze that came laden with the perfume of peaceful fields, under the canopy of the deep blue heavens, listened to the oration of the Hon. Charles L. Remond. The exercises opened with prayer by one of our citizens, invoking the blessings of heaven upon all. After which Mr. Remond proceeded in a most able and eloquent manner to review, in fine style, the most important incidents connected with the event we had met to celebrate. His theme was: "The Advancement of the Colored People." He referred to the present condition and future prospects of my people. Every word was sparkling, brilliant, convincing and touching, and was received with great applause. His speech was full of thoughts that breathe, and words that burn, and was listened to with marked attention and interest.

After the address was a collation, to which the people did ample justice. The long tables were arranged with much taste, by competent ladies, and others, who had them in charge. It was an enjoyable occasion for every one present. The Norwich Brass Band played in fine style the pleasing national airs; among them were "Hail, Columbia," and the "Star Spangled Banner," which always stir up the patriotism of every true American, and were loudly encored. It was an event long to be remembered in the hearts of my people, and is one of the greatest and brightest events that has ever occurred in our history as a people, and should be handed down from generation to generation. We tender our thanks to the citizens of Norwich, for their generosity and kindness in aiding us in that great and good cause.

In Memoriam

The Hon. Charles L. Remond is no more, for his earthly career is ended. By his untiring energy he became one of our first men, and advanced, step by step, till he became a custom house officer at Boston. His well-known qualifications as a man were more than of ordinary mark, and well-fitted him for the position and duties which he was called to fill. He always wielded his pen for the benefit of his people. As an orator, he has had few equals. His pen has carried light and comfort to many a household of my people. He was one of the pioneers of the anti-slavery movement in its earliest days, when agitation was at its height. Let his honored name be held in grateful remembrance, to be handed down from posterity to posterity.

Dear reader, this simple story of my life is no record of bold events, that, with the multitude constitute the hero; no tell tale of fiction to draw on the imagination. It is a story that is real, that is earnest; and if it touches the simple heart that has power to sympathize with the unfortunate in times of adversity, and to mingle in the joys that come to the after-life, giving peace and satisfaction to the soul, it will accomplish its purpose. I have hesitated in this work, feeling that ordinarily the experiences of the individual life are sacred, and that the bitterest and the best belong to one's own self, and can never be felt by another. But there are lives whose experiences the public have a right to know; lives wrought out in the interest of some great cause, or so linked to the progress of humanity that they modify and mould its destiny. The life that is buoyant with hope, living perpetually in God's sunshine, realizing every thing that is sweet in existence, has little in it that touches the chord of sympathy, and no necessity calls for its revealment. Yet there are those in toils and trials that reap an experience that, when made known, unfold a lesson of admonition and comfort to others. Life's ways, in this regard, are so mysterious, that we are dumb to the inquiry: "Why is it so?" Yet, flowing out of this, we see the Guiding Hand preparing us for better things, moulding us for a better life. The slave-life of which this little volume so largely treats is analogous to this.

No mystery was ever deeper than that which shrouds the path by which men were led into bondage, and no system was ever more cruel and intolerant than that which inflicted stripes and burdens upon men, without cause, and deprived them of liberty and the right to life. Yet when we look back upon God's dealings with his early people, and see how they wrought in bondage and suffered in their wanderings from it, it reveals His power of bringing good out of evil, light out of darkness, and becomes a school of wisdom to the world. So the first slave ship that crossed the ocean, with its stolen fruits of life and liberty, of bone and muscle, of sinew and nerve, of flesh and spirit, bore tidings of sorrow and wretchedness to generations, whom, yet through the darkness and gloom of two centuries the Great Disposer of all events saw the end. We are yet unable to see it. The wail of the bondmen toiling in the brake, or under the scourging lash must have a significance in the work of civilization, or God is not wise or just.

The filling up of their years with misery and degradation must mean something more than an event of fate, else there is no law of progress that bears men on through storm, tumult and tempest to the goal of peace. We are just crossing the bitter waters, and can scarcely see our landing; we are not safe over, yet we hope to escape the storms that are still beating upon us, and moor our bark on the shore of freedom. Dear friend, read this simple story carefully, and ponder its lessons. What if it had been your child, stolen from your home, borne to a foreign shore, doomed to such a life, and destined to become the progenitor of a race bound to toil and woe, would not your heart flow in sympathy with the weakest of that race who should come to you in sorrow? But, say you, the day of trial is over, the stream of sympathy may be dried up because of the nominal freedom that has been vouchsafed. I say to you nay; my whole race is yet in peril, and God only knows the end. The love of gain, the lust of power is still dominant, and ceases not to inflict their burdens and enforce their demands.

Sorrowing at the situation, pained at the necessity which yet drives our brethren from pillar to post, or binds them to the wicked caprices of their old masters, yet we appreciate the open hearts that welcome them to new homes, and the willing hands that minister to their dire necessities. We have yet much to ask of others; we have much more to accomplish for ourselves. What has been wrought in the past cannot be overcome at once. Gradually the work of demoralization does its work, and not much swifter must be the work of regeneration. We cannot save ourselves without aid and sympathy from others; without the protection of just laws and righteous judgment; others cannot save us without our aid—without the consecration of all our best faculties to the work before us. Let us, then, work mutually in unfolding the mysteries of that Providence which is not only bringing us up out of bondage, but which is to redeem the whole race of mankind from the gloom of darkness and the thralldom of sin.

With these thoughts I leave, asking you to give your hearts to wisdom, restraining yourselves from selfishness, and living for the good of others. There has been enough of pain, and sorrow, and despair. The whole current of life must be changed, and men be taught no longer to hedge the way of others, but to scatter sunbeams, solar sunbeams; the sunbeams of life in their path.

X COLORED MEN DURING THE WAR

In battle—Kindness to Union men—Devotion to the Union—29th Conn.—Its departure—Return—The noble Kansas troops—54th Mass.—Obedient to orders.

It is a fact to be lamented that the historians of our country speak so little about the heroic deeds of the colored troops; in fact, by some no mention is made of them at all; but, let it be as it may, the fact that they, after many petitions to be allowed to take their place in the ranks, fought bravely and well, lives in the heart of every true American citizen. Many were the commendations they received from their officers. Look at them at Fort Pillow, Milliken's Bend, Port Hudson, Fort Wagner, and Olustee! Where do we find them? In places of most imminent danger, where the battle raged hottest, closing up where their ranks were thinned out before a reeking fire of grape and canister.

"Cannon to the right of them!
Cannon to the left of them!
Onward they went,
'Noble black regiment!'"

The black man went into the war with but one determination: that once learning the use of arms, he would never again be made a slave. Whether he ever enjoyed the blessed privileges of freedom himself it mattered little to him so that his race derived the benefits. Says one officer: "I never saw men more willing to sacrifice themselves on the 'altar of their country' than those in the 8th U.S., of which I have command." Says a captain of another colored company: "I never saw a more heroic company of men in my life." And thus it might be said of many other colored regiments that went into the field. None were ever known to flee when the hour of battle was nigh; nay, rather it was as much as the officers could do to restrain them till the order to fire should be given.

The slaves had it in their power, when their masters were away to the war, to kill their defenceless wives and children, many of whom had been left in their care. How often has the case been when the master, just before leaving his home, has called to him his most faithful servant and left in his charge those most dear to him; and I have known cases where silverware and other valuables have been stowed away in some old cabin till "mar's comes back." Ah! the slave-holder knew the slaves could be trusted—a fact which the North was not long in finding out, even before it tried the experiment of organizing them into troops.

A Union soldier being wounded, probably left in the woods to die, having wandered about under cover of night, at last falls upon the cabin of some old "aunty." A sense of safety and security steals over him, for he knows that no power on earth could make her betray him. I copy an extract of a letter, showing the kindness of the slaves towards the Union soldiers, to which many of them can testify:

"ADVENTURES OF TWO ESCAPED PRISONERS, AND THE
HELP THEY RECEIVED FROM THE SLAVES IN THE PERILOUS
VOYAGE THENCE TO KNOXVILLE, TENNESSEE.

"Two Union officers, Lieut. Col. Thomas J. Leigh, of the
71st New York, and Lieut. Tincker, of Indiana, had made
their escape from the prison stockade at Columbia, S.C.
They traveled two nights, and got within three miles of
Lexington, when they met a couple of slaves, and asked
them the direction to Ninety-Six Station. They pointed
out to the officers the road, and asserted positively that
'they were their friends, and when they wanted assistance
they must crawl up to the fields about dusk, and wait for
a field hand to come along; that they would furnish them
with provisions, and never betray them.' On the fifth
night of their journey they were making north-west for
Knoxville, Tenn. On the evening of the sixth day they
ventured cautiously to a plantation where they saw a
large number of hogs in a field running toward them as
though they expected to be fed, and they judged from
this that a slave would soon come and feed them. They
were right in their conjecture, for in a few moments a
slave came along with a basket on his head, with corn for
the hogs. Col. Leigh called to him, and, as he came up to
him, questioned him 'if he would betray him?' The slave
replied: 'No; the negroes in that part of the country did
not do that sort of thing.' He said: 'You must be hungry?'
The officer replied: 'That was what I hailed you for.' The
slave advised him 'to wait about an hour, and he'll have
lots to eat.' He then started for the house, and in about an
hour came back, along with several other slaves, all carrying eatables—chicken, possum, rice and shortcake—
sufficient to last a two days' journey. As it began to rain,
the slaves advised them 'to lay still that night, and it
would clear up before morning.' Both of the officers took
their advice, and they kept them company all night.

"They were very anxious about the state of affairs. They asked the officers 'if they thought Jeff. Davis was going to give the slaves arms;' and then said that their 'masters had made propositions to them, that if they would take up arms and fight for the South, they would be free.' One of the officers asked them 'if they would fight against the North?' They promptly replied: 'Only let them give us arms, and we will show them which side we will fight for.' They said: 'We have now some arms hid;' and wanted to know 'if, when they were formed into companies and regiments, whether they could be together, and talk with one another.' He told them 'Certainly.' One slave remarked: 'My master offers me my freedom if I will take up arms, but I have a family—a wife and five children—and he does not offer to free them; and we have come to the conclusion that there is no use in fighting for our freedom when any one of our children we may have are to be made slaves.' He felt that he could not himself enjoy the blessings of freedom while his own wife and children toiled in hopeless bondage. Continued he: 'When we get the use of arms, and are permitted to be together in regiments, we can demand freedom for our families, and take it.' Another one remarked 'that their masters did not venture to whip them now; that they were fed on a little better food than before the war, and they believed this was only done so humor them and keep them quiet.'

"They departed the next morning, wishing the slaves 'good luck,' and they replying 'God bless you,' which is a very common expression in that portion of the country. They then pursued their journey, without anything worthy of note happening, until they arrived in the Pickens District, S.C., on a plantation of Dr. Earl, who was publicly known to be a secessionist. Here they were in the midst of a large number of slaves of his plantation, and others, discussing the arrival of Gen. Sherman, at Augusta, Ga.

"It appeared that they had in a secret manner sent one of their number in haste towards Hamburg, to get fresh information about Sherman, with the intention, on the arrival of the courier, to make a general stampede into the Union lines. They counted on between five and eight thousand slaves, who consented to go with them. All of these men treated the officers very kindly, and gave them a large supply of provisions. They told them 'to stop at the home of John W. Wilson, a strong Union man.' Accordingly, the next evening about half-past nine o'clock, Col. Leigh knocked at Wilson's door; he came, holding a revolver in his hand, and demanded to know who they were. They told him that 'they were escaped Union officers.' After hearing this, he invited them into his house, and treated them very cordially. He informed them of the re-election of President Lincoln, and as they were about leaving him, went kindly with them to the middle of the road, where they all gave three cheers for Abraham Lincoln.

"Being properly directed on their course, they reached Bumcomb County, in Western North Carolina. There they saw a woman in the field plowing; she informed them that in that County, and also in Henderson and Madison Counties, there were over five hundred men who had been conscripted—enrolled militiamen—her husband among the number, who, refusing to join the Confederate army, lay concealed in caves in the woods. The country is ransacked by Rebel details, who plunder the defenceless women and children, and shoot the men if found in the woods. In traveling over a distance of one hundred and thirty miles, across the mountains, a scene of great destitution prevailed; women performed the duties of men; the children had no shoes, and the country seemed given up to entire lawlessness. The remainder of their journey was executed solely under the guidance of women, and on the evening of December

13th they reached Knoxville, having spent forty-four days in their perilous travels."

Many a soldier has been carefully nursed by slaves, and sent back to the army a well man. It will be seen, moreover, that the slave was no respecter of persons, as in this instance. A slave mother, who, on bidding her son "God speed," on his way to the war, exclaimed: "If you see Mar's, pick him out de fust one." The name "Yankee," to these poor, depressed people meant freedom, and they were never known to turn their hand against a blue-coat.

At the beginning of the war many black men went as servants, and at times of battle begged for a bayonet, and took their places in a company. How many brave souls perished this way will never be known till the judgment. History has made no note of them, though they died riddled with bullets, with the bayonet grasped firmly in the hand.

Some of the slave-holders offered their slaves freedom if they would join the Confederate army. Says one: "I have a wife and children in slavery; he don't say a word about freeing them. No, sir, I don't fight unless they can be free, too." Others, on being interrogated as "to what they'd do if arms were put in their hands, whether they would fight for the South," replied: "Let them give us arms, we'll show them which side we fight for." And so, at last, when the experiment was tried, whether the black man would run in battle, it was soon found out which side they were determined to fight for.

As soon as it was made known that colored volunteers would be accepted they came pouring in from all sections. In Norwich a regiment was soon formed, (29th Conn.,) which did good service in the field. Never did we feel prouder than when, after a few weeks' encampment in New

Haven, they marched away with flying banners and martial music.

Some of the ladies of color instituted a Ladies' Aid Society, which met once a week at the houses of its different members to make up both fancy and useful articles, as they intended to hold a fair in one the largest halls in the place—the proceeds of which were to be devoted to getting up a box for the brave 29th. There was in it almost every conceivable delicacy that could be imagined, that would bring delight to any one far away from home and longing for its luxuries. There were also useful and needy articles, put up by loving hands, for the brave boys who had given their lives for their country. Some few of them lived to return. In the severe fighting before Petersburg many found an early grave.

The fair was held for one week, at Breed Hall, which was most handsomely decorated with flags and banners. The tables were arranged around the halls, and fairly crowded upon them were articles of every description. Many thanks are due to those who so well patronized us. Many influential families sent in contributions, both of money and articles to help the cause. Too much can not be said of the members of the society for their untiring zeal—how they met, through storm and rain—nothing deterred them from their work. If, at times, their spirits seemed to flag, thoughts of the brave 29th, at their dangerous post, stirred them up with renewed vigor. The fair netted a handsome profit. The box was quickly made ready, and sent on its way.

We have the surety that the box reached its destination, from the following extract of a letter written by E.C. Green, to an officer of the regiment. It reads thus:

★   ★   ★ "Before closing may I refer you to the pleasure you gave to the ladies of our Soldiers' Aid Society, a year since in allowing them to furnish your regiment with a box of hospital supplies, and say to you, if your supplies are at present insufficient, we would be glad to forward another box of similar articles, if your surgeon would have the pleasure of sending us a list of articles needed. With much esteem,

Yours, very truly,
E.C. Green."

Departure of the Brave
Twenty-ninth Conn.

At two P.M. the regiment stood in waiting. A few moments after, a carriage containing Major General Russell, Major Tyler, Major Wayland, and Alderman Marble, drove up in front of the regiment; every man of which stood erect and manly as if conscious of what was before him. A handsome flag was presented by Miss Diantha Hodge, to whom Col. Wooster responded in a soldier like speech; after which the order was given, and they marched off by the right flank, amid the cheers of the assembled crowds, and the farewells of old friends. Cheer after cheer came from the lips of the men as they saw the stars and stripes floating to the breeze along the line of march. The regiment halted on the old Green for an hour, waiting for the tide to rise to enable the steamer Warrior to near the wharf, then the line of march was resumed down Chapel Street to State, down State to the wharf. At six o'clock, the regiment marched on board, with orders to report at the depot of the ninth army corps, at Annapolis, Md.

Reaching this place they found themselves anything but comfortable—a sharp, raw north-east wind prevailing. The tents did not arrive till nearly dark; these were hastily pitched and occupied. In the morning they awoke to find themselves covered with from one to three feet of snow. Crackling, blazing camp-fires were built, and around them cheerful blue coated dark skins gathered, full of wit and humor. On the 27th of April, 1864, the regiment left for the front. Its sufferings in the bloody struggle before Richmond were terrible and heart rending. It went into the fight of eleven hours with four hundred and fifty brave, armed and equipped men; it came out with one hundred and eighty men, all told—no field officers, and one wounded company officer.

Their Return

On the morning of Oct. 14th, 1865, orders were received to prepare to be mustered out of the U.S. service. Oct. 16th the boys bade good-bye to hard-tack, salt horse, and other delicacies known nowhere but in the army. They embarked on board the steamer, singing "Homeward Bound." After reaching New York they embarked for Hartford, where they would be paid off, and receive their discharge papers. Here they were met by the Mayor and a committee, and marched up to Central Row, headed by Colt's Brass Band, where they stacked arms and unslung knapsacks; then the battalion formed in two ranks and marched to the City Hall, where a splendid feast awaited them.

On entering the hall the first thing to be seen was the "Star Spangled Benner," extended across the hall, and in the centre a banner bearing the following: "Welcome, 29th C.V.;" "Deep Bottom," "Strawberry Plains, Va.," "Siege of Petersburg," "New Market Heights," "Danberry Town Road," "Chapin's Farm," "Fair Oaks." At the head of the banner was an evergreen wreath, prepared by ladies. On the stand were the busts of Lincoln, and others.

After feasting, they were ordered to march to Central Row, where they learned the 31st U.S.C.I. had just arrived. The 29th and 31st then formed in a square on State House Square, where they were addressed by Mayor Stillman; afterwards, by His Excellency, Gov. Buckingham. After a few remarks from Col. Wooster and Gen. Hawley, the 31st were escorted to the City Hall, where a breakfast awaited them. The 29th were then dismissed.

The Noble Kansas Troops

On the 29th of Oct., 1862, twenty-four men of the 1st Regiment of Kansas, Colored Volunteers, having advanced beyond the limits prescribed, were charged upon by one hundred and twenty of the Rebel cavalry. There was a desperate hand-to-hand encounter. There was no flinching; no hesitating; no trembling of limb. Each man saw exactly how matters stood, and, with calm precision, made every stroke tell. Finally re-inforcements came up. Out of the twenty-four men, only six escaped unhurt. The Rebels were armed with shot-guns, revolvers and sabres; our men with Austrian rifles and sabre bayonets. This last is a fearful weapon, and did terrible execution. Six Killer, the leader of the Cherokee negroes, shot two men, bayoneted a third, and laid the fourth with the butt of his gun. Another was attacked by three men. He discharged his rifle and had no time to load again. When asked to surrender, he replied by a stunning blow from the butt of his rifle, which knocked the Rebel off his horse.

So ended the battle of Island Mounds, which resulted in a complete victory to the negro regiment. It has been found out that black men make splendid soldiers—that they are anxious to serve their country and their race. No one can point the finger of scorn at the Kansas troops and say they were cowards; yet four months passed and they were not mustered—still they adhered to their organization through every discouragement and disadvantage. Chances of recognition were slim. They demanded of the military authorities to be either accepted or disbanded.

The 1st North Carolina Regiment was commanded by Col. James C. Beecher, brother of the Rev. H.W. Beecher. Their camp was on the south side of the Neuse River. The ground had been enclosed by the men so that the locality presented quite a neat appearance. Col. Beecher thus writes to his friends:

> ★　★　★　"I wish doubtful people at home could see my three weeks' regiment. They would talk less nonsense about negro inferiority. Our discipline is to-day better than that of any regiment I know of; and I believe, by the blessing of God, our efficiency will be second to none."

A little later he says:

> ★　★　★　"My regiment is a 'buster,' improves every day; and such a line of battle as we form! It would make your eyes shine to see these six weeks' soldiers going through a dress parade. A month later the regiment is considered ready for a fair fight."

Towards the last of July they left Newbern for Charlestown, and were put to digging trenches, getting only a lull occasionally on the beach by moonlight. It was quite a romantic scene: the hard, white beach; the ocean waves splashing along the sand; the long line of black soldiers, their guns shining in the moonlight. They had a great desire to learn; and, although the digging went on, the officers would instruct them at night in the speller, so that before they went to Florida three hundred of them had learned to read and write.

Much has been said about the bravery of the 54th Mass. On one occasion it saved a whole brigade from being captured or annihilated. The lamented Col. Shaw was one of its commanders. At Fort Wagner, when the color sergeant fell, and our flag would have been trailing in the dust, one of its noble boys seized it, sprang upon the parapet, where he received three severe wounds. When the order was given to retire, the noble color bearer still held the flag in the air; and, with the assistance of his comrades, succeeded in reaching the hospital, where he fell exhausted, saying: "The old flag never touched the ground, boys."

There was a great deal of murmuring among the friends of the regiment in Boston, because of statements reaching them that it was called upon to perform more than its proportional part of dangerous duty; and this seems true, since, in the most perilous places there would be found the glorious 54th.

I mention a few facts to show that the slaves were so accustomed to obeying orders that they would follow out any instructions to the very letter. It is said that while Gen. Grant was walking along the dock, smoking, a colored guard came up to him and said: "No smoking on this dock, sir." The General looked at him and said: "Were those your orders?" "Yes, sir." "Very good orders," replied the General, smiling, and throwing his cigar into the water. Again, a Rebel picket offered a large piece of tobacco to a colored sentinel if he would give him one biscuit, or hard-tack as it is called. "Against orders to exchange with you Rebs," he replied, and no entreaties would cause him to swerve one iota from his instructions.

A Reb. was found by two colored pickets skulking outside the Union lines. How he cursed and swore when he found that he must be brought into camp under the surveillance of two black soldiers. He refused to stir one step; "he'd die on the spot first." "Just as you please," replied the guard, "we take you, dead or alive." The Reb. raved the more, and said: "It was enough to make his father rise up out of his grave." When last seen he was marching into camp at the point of the bayonet.

In consequence of the breaking of the Weldon R.R. by Grant, much of the Rebel munitions of war and supplies had to be run over a distance of sixteen miles, and then transferred to the cars. Every thing that could be used for carrying purposes was pressed into their service. Horses and mules were scarce in the Confederacy, so, in many instances, negroes were hitched to the wagons, and it was said made better time than when horses were used. They would go on their way, singing and joking; and, after a half-hour's intermission at certain places, would push onward as fresh and lively as ever.

The slaves were of great assistance to the Union army on account of their thorough knowledge of the country: its ways and resources: its wood, water, fuel, game: and also of the habits of the enemy. Nothing escaped them. They'd tell today what happened yesterday thirty miles off; would risk their lives to give any information which was to be of advantage to the Union.

At Washington the contrabands, as they were termed during the war, knew every inch of ground between there and Richmond, and gave valuable information for maps, engineering parties and reconnoissances. Contraband pioneers, armed with sharp axes, would go on expeditions through the woods, under cover of the carbines of the cavalry, hewing away the heavy timber, and preparing the road for the advance. Every thing in the shape of a dog was killed. About the plantations could be seen the lifeless bodies of bloodhounds whose deep baying would no longer be heard about the swamps, indicating the close proximity of pursuers.

XI | RECOLLECTIONS OF THE WAR

The spirit of the South—Delaware—Kentucky—
Meetings—Conventions—Gen. Wild's raid—
Slave heroism—A reminiscence of 1863—Sherman's
march through Georgia—Arming the slave.

The spirit of the rebellion still shows itself in many of the States. Its influences are plainly manifested in the State of Delaware. In my escape from the South I passed through this State. How I ever succeeded, without being detected, I can not tell to this day. Nothing but the mercy of the Lord ever carried me through. Here, in the height of slavery, I went on board the boat at New Castle, and no white man questioned me as to my whereabouts, or asked for my pass. As for the town of New Castle, the very atmosphere seemed tainted with slavery.

The feeling was most bitter in Odessa, during 1865, against persons of color from the North giving lectures in the town. On one occasion a mob of white ruffians surrounded a colored church, showering stones and bricks at the doors and windows, swearing that the meeting should be dismissed. One of the local laws of the State says that: "Any negro or mulatto coming into the State, who is a non-resident of the locality he may visit, is liable to a fine of fifty dollars, six month's imprisonment, and twenty-five lashes." Learning of this, they concluded to dismiss the meeting.

March 4th, 1865, Maj. Gen. Palmer issued an order that: "All slave pens, and other private establishments for confining persons in Louisville, be suppressed; and all confined persons discharged, except such as have committed crimes." A colored police officer brought out many an innocent man and woman. Some had iron bars on their legs, reaching from the hip to the ankle and fastened on with iron straps.

There was a time in the history of Kentucky when colored men, women and children found upon the highways after dark were surrounded by the city guard, and flogged by them in the public streets. In Louisville the Rev. Mr. James called a meeting at which delegates were appointed to hold an interview with the President, calling his attention to a few of the laws which bore so heavily on our race: First, they had no oath; second, they had no right of domicile; third, no right of locomotion; fourth, no right of self-defense; fifth, a statute of Kentucky makes it a penal crime, with imprisonment in the penitentiary for one year, for any freeman of color, under any circumstances, to pass into a free State, even for a moment. Any freeman, not a native, found within her borders is subject to the same penalty; and for the second offense shall be a slave for life.

In 1865 the first delegation of colored men that ever left Kentucky, on a mission of liberty, started for Washington to accomplish the noble work entrusted to their hands. The interview was satisfactory, the President assuring them that the government would yield them every protection, and that the martial law would continue till the Kentuckians should learn more truly their position, and their duty to the nation.

The first free convention in the State of Virginia, during a period of two hundred and fifty-five years, was held in Alexandria, at the Lyceum Building. Fifty delegates were present. Addresses were made by Geo. W. Cook, of Norfolk; Peter R. Jones, of Petersburg; and Nicholas Richmond, of Charlottesville.

The Celebration of the Fourth of July in Louisville, Kentucky

For the first time the people celebrated this day as a free people. Extensive preparations were made. There was a great out-pouring of people. They came from the factories, the work-shops and the fields to enjoy themselves in the pure, fresh air of freedom. The procession was formed in the following manner:

123rd U.S.C.I.—eight hundred strong.
Band.
Fifth St. Sabbath School—Asbury Chapel S.S.—Quinn
Chapel
S.S.—Jackson St. S.S.—Green St. S.S.—
York St. S.S.—Centre St. S.S.
Band.
Government Employees, one hundred and fifty—
Sons of Union—
West Union Sons—Sons of Honor—United Brothers
of Friendship—United Fellows.
Car tastefully decorated, drawn by four horses, filled
with misses,
representing the Fifth St. Baptist Aid Society.

Car representing the Original Aid Society in Kentucky.
The Colored Ladies' Soldier's and Freedman's Aid
Society.
Car filled with working men, plying the saw, plane,
hammer and mallet.
125th U.S.C.I.—six hundred strong.
Band.

Fully ten thousand persons marched in the procession, and ten thousand more assembled on the ground. A sumptuous dinner was prepared for the soldiers, after which the speaking began. Addresses were made by David Jenkins, J.M. Langston, Chaplain Collins and Lieut. Ward. When Gen. Palmer appeared such a shout as went up was enough to bring all the invisible sprites and spirits from their hiding places. As soon as it became quiet he began. His speech was continually applauded. He finished amid rounds of applause, banners waving, and the band playing the "Star Spangled Banner." That night the heavens were ablaze with rockets, fiery serpents and blue lights.

Gen. Wild's Raid

During a march, when our troops neared a plantation, the slaves would eagerly join them. In many instances in plundering the houses slaves were found locked up. Continually during this raiding expedition, slaves came pouring in from the country in every direction, with their household furniture, thronging the lately deserted streets. This expedition was to search out guerrillas, lurking about the neighborhood of Elizabeth City and firing on our pickets. A force of colored men fell on their camp. There was a hasty escapade, and the soldiers came in possession of fire-arms and horses.

Leaving Elizabeth City, they passed by vast fields of corn a mile in extent, commodious looking buildings and magnificent plantations. Here the troops commenced to work in earnest, and became an army of liberation.

On the first plantation they found fourteen slaves, who gladly joined them. An old wagon was found, to which a horse was harnessed. Such furniture as the slaves needed was placed in it, and the women and children on top. And so they went from house to house, gathering together the slaves, and whatever teams and horses could be found. Meanwhile, foraging went on, as there was an abundance of geese, chicken and turkeys. All the planters were "Secesh," so no restrictions were placed on the troops. The line of march continued, the contraband train continually growing in length.

At Indian Town bridge Gen. Wild came upon a guerrilla camp. His men started upon the "double quick," and pursed them through woods, across corn fields, until they came to a swamp. Here no path whatever could be seen, and how the guerrillas succeeded in covering their flight was, at first, a mystery; but our men were in for it now, and did not intend to turn back before ferreting out the matter. They began a careful search, and soon found the trunk of a felled tree, well-worn with footsteps. Near by was another, then another till they made quite a zig-zag footpath across the swamp. This solved the mystery. This, without doubt, led to the guerrilla quarters. Going single file they came upon a small island, which had been hastily evacuated—every thing was lying about in great confusion. According to orders, the soldiers burned the huts and took possession of whatever was worth keeping. The slaves on the plantations, ahead of the line, were notified by scouts to be ready to join the train when it should pass. By the time it reached Currituck Court

House it was a mile in length. After three weeks the entire expedition returned to Norfolk. The raid was considered a very important one.

The tables were now turned. Those proud-hearted planters, who claimed such strict obedience from their slaves, now actually fell down on their knees before these armed blacks and begged for their lives. The great cry among them was: "What shall I do to be saved?" Yes, now they were ready to take the oath of allegiance, give up their slaves; any thing "to be saved." Whole families ran to the swamps when they heard that the raiders were near.

This raid put at rest forever the question as to whether the negro troops were efficient in any part of the service. They performed all the duties of white soldiers—scouting, skirmishing, picket duty, guard duty; and, lastly, fighting. Gen. Wild had decided at one time to attack a guerrilla camp. With the exception of thirty-five men, who were too lame to march, every man wanted to go and fight the guerrillas, notwithstanding those could remain back who wished to guard the camp. No persuasions could induce them to volunteer to remain; so at last Gen. Wild was obliged to detail the required number for this duty. Did any one ever think that the men who had been accustomed to hunt runaway slaves in the swamps of the South would now be hiding there themselves, be hunted by them? Mysterious are thy ways, Oh, Lord!

When the rebellion first broke out a great many people thought "now the slaves will make a grand rush for the Northern side." They had prayed so long for liberty. Here it was, right in their hand; but the slaves did n't do any such thing. Remaining quiet, and looking about to see how things on both sides were moving, was the very means that saved them. How were they to contend with their masters? They had no arms, nothing to fight with; their masters had been collecting implements of war for some time and the slaves knew it; knew where they were hid; knew all the lines of fortification which they had been compelled to construct. Ah, the slaves were too wise to run any risk, with nothing but hoes in their hands. They said nothing, saw every thing, and at the right time they would give the Union valuable information. The Rebels lost their cause, and why? Because the slaves were loyal to the government. If they had been disloyal, the Confederates would no doubt have won, or else some foreign power might have intervened and made trouble. As it is, the Rebs. owe an old grudge to the freedman, as much as to say: "Its your fault we didn't win."

Heroism of a Contraband

It was just after the victory of the Excelsior Brigade at Fair Oaks, when Gen. Sickels received word that the enemy were advancing. Orders for preparation for battle were given. At last all was in readiness for the advance; but only a few shots were to be heard in the distance, otherwise every thing was quiet. What did it mean? The General asked Lieutenant Palmer to take a squad of men with him and ride cautiously to the first bend in the road, but he, too impetuous, rushed daringly ahead till he was within range of the enemy. He fell, pierced with bullets. His soldiers hastily retreated to their camp and told their news. Among the listeners was a negro servant of Lieut. Palmer, who quietly withdrew and walked down that road—that road of death—for after passing our picket guard he was openly exposed to the

Rebel sharpshooters. When our soldiers came up, the faithful servant was found by the side of his dead master. I regret that the name of this heroic soul remains unknown to the world—a name worthy to be emblazoned on the pages of history.

We used often to hear the question asked, can the negro take care of himself? If he is set free, to rely on his own resources, will he not die of starvation? Let us see. At Pine Bluffs there was a full black, known as Uncle Reuben. He was born in Georgia, and displayed such energy, tact, and devotion to his master's interest that he was left in full charge of every thing on the plantation. The slave raised his master from poverty to wealth. At last his master died, and his widow depended still more upon Uncle Reuben, placing all in his hands. He became more ambitious, and succeeded so well that the number of cotton bales increased every year. The children were sent North to school. The white overseers became jealous of him, and compelled his mistress to place a white, nominally, over him. However, he was not interfered with and his mistress treated him as kindly as she dared. Then the sons returned from the North, with no feelings of gratitude to one who by his industry and prudence had educated them, and amassed a fortune of one hundred and fifty thousand dollars. Thank God, he lived to see freedom's light, and after being assured that the Proclamation was a fact, he came over to us.

A Reminiscence of 1863

Probably no act—the Ku Klux system excepted—was more distressing than the ever to-be-remembered riot which occurred in New York city during the year of 1863. (The mob spirit first manifested itself at a meeting held in Boston, December 3rd, 1860, in observance of the anniversary of the death of John Brown.) I can but look back and shudder at that great carnival of blood. The mob commenced on the 10th of July, and continued day and night for more than a week. My heart aches when memory recalls that awful day, when the whole city was in a state of insurrection. The full force of the infuriated mob fell upon the black man, the harmless, unpretending black man, whose only crime was that his skin was of a darker hue than his white brethren; that he came of a race which for more than two hundred years has felt the sting of slavery in its very soul. I know of no race that has undergone more sufferings than the black race in America.

Brought here from our mother country, we have bedewed the soil with our blood and tears. Unlike the Indian, we leave vengeance to the Lord. "He will repay." In this riot hundreds of colored people were driven from their homes, hunted and chased through the streets like wild beasts. A sweet babe was brained while holding up his little arms, and smiling upon his murderers. Many little children were killed in this manner. Strong men were dragged from their home and left dangling from some lamp post or tree, or else slaughtered on the streets—their blood flowing in streams down the pavements. Able-bodied men, whose mangled bodies hung up to lamp posts, were in a great many instances burned to cinders. The colored people were panic stricken and sought shelter in out-of-the-way nooks and places; but even then some were discovered by the mob on their way to a retreat and quickly dispatched; hundreds flocked to the floors of police stations, prisons and jails, and begged admittance. No colored man, woman or child was spared if found. As a general thing, colored tenants occupy whole streets, so the mob knew pretty well what localities to plunder. Pistol shots were fired through the windows, murdering many at their homes and by their firesides. This accounts for the great loss of life, greater than if the people lived more scattered. The police were not able to cope with the murderers, though it is believed they did what they could, going in companies of two or three hundred to such parts of the city as needed their protection most. A most heartless transaction committed by these fiends, was the destruction of the colored Orphan Asylum, after first robbing the little children of their clothing. These helpless lambs were driven friendless upon the world from the burning Asylum, which had been their abode. The mob went on at a terrible rate.

My family were quietly seated at the table one bright July morning when we were startled by the sudden ringing of the door bell. Upon responding, we found that a family with whom we were well acquainted had succeeded in escaping from the city, and sought refuge in our quiet suburb until quietness and peace should reign, so as to enable them to return to their own home. Oh! ye people of the North, before you censure too strongly the actions of the South, rid your own soil of that fiendish element which makes it an opprobrium to call America "the land of the free and the home of the brave."

Sherman's March Through Georgia

During Sherman's march from Atlanta to Savannah, many thousands of slaves came into the ranks, all of whom appeared overjoyed that "de Yanks. had come." It would often happen that he would encamp on the plantations that planters had deserted. Here would be found an abundance of the good things of this life, of which the soldiers would readily partake. At one place only the old, decrepit slaves were left. These were half naked, and nearly starved; they had been told frightful stories about the cruelties of the Yankee soldiers, and were as frightened as could be when the army arrived. Upon being reassured that no harm would be done them, they were overwhelming in their thanks to Gen. Sherman for clothing and feeding them.

And thus it was; all along the march the most pathetic scenes would occur. Thousands of women, carrying household goods, some with children in their arms, all anxious to join the column. When refused, some most heart-rending scene would take place; such begging to be allowed to go on to Savannah, where, says one: "My chillens done been sold dese four years;" or to Macon to "see my boy." Gen. Sherman, with great tact, succeeded in quieting them, telling them they would return for them some day and they must be patient. An aged couple had been waiting sixty years for deliverance. No one to see them at work on the plantation would suppose that they were any thing but satisfied with their condition. No murmur, no words of discontent ever passed their lips; they made no comments on the actions of runaway slaves; their master had no fears for them; yet, could he have seen the face of the woman when she heard that the Yankees had come, he would have seen that he had not read her heart aright. Such an expression as her countenance assumed was terrible to behold. "Bress de Lord," she exclaimed, "I expects to follow them till I drop in my tracks." As her husband did not see the situation of things as quickly as she did, she angrily said: "What are you sitting dar fur, don't yer see de door open? I'se not waited sixty years for nuttin'." It is said that no persuasion would prevail upon her to remain where she had suffered so much, and old as she was she would follow the army. This is only one of the many hundred cases which constantly occurred during the war. This poorly enlightened people all seemed to think that the Yankees would come some time or other, and that their freedom was the object of the war. This notion, I suppose, they got from hearing their masters talk.

The Rebel leaders had their attention completely absorbed by the vast preparations they were making for carrying on the war, by the increasing of State debts, etc. The question of arming the slaves, which had been warmly debated at Richmond, was overlooked. The governors of the several Southern States had also pondered this question as the only means to save the Confederacy, which under its various reverses, was slowly but surely dying. The South knew it could not hold out much longer. An intelligent mulatto in Macon, Ga., who used to attend his master's store would often make mention of such conversation as he overheard between his master and some of the first men of the city. They used to get together in the counting-room and say: "It was no use to fight the North any longer; the South would surely be whipped in the end, and the best thing that could be done, would be to fix up the old Union." When asked if these men talked so on the public street, he replied: "No sir," these very men would go out on the street and talk wild about "whipping the Yankees, the South never giving up, and a lot of other trash." It is said that the Rebels so frightened their slaves, telling them stories of the cruelties which would be practiced upon them if ever they put themselves in the power of the Yankees that the most ignorant knew scarcely which way to turn, when the question of arming the slaves was discussed. There was nothing said by the South about the reward for their services. It rather looked upon them in the same light as when they worked in the field; neither was it prepared to meet the various objections raised by the white soldiers, if compelled to fight with them, side by side. So, as all parties could not be satisfied, the matter was allowed to drop, though I have no doubt but that to save herself, a few would have been willing to have increased their forces, by accepting the assistance of the slave.

XII | THE EXODUS

*Arrival of negroes in Washington—Hospitality of
Washington people—Suffering and privation—Education
of the freedmen—Causes of emigration—Cruelty at the
South—Prejudice at the North—Hopes for the future.*

The Rebellion at length closed after a bloody carnage of about four years. The manacles of the slave had been burst asunder. Left in abject poverty, he is suddenly thrown upon his own resources for support. In many instances the ex-slaveholder employed his former slaves on his plantation, paying them certain wages; others hired their own ground, and being perfectly familiar with the raising of cotton, sugar, corn and other grain, succeeded in making quite a comfortable living and having something laid by "for a rainy day." But this was not to last long. The peace of the quiet villages and towns was soon disturbed by night-raiders. Law-abiding citizens were torn from their beds at midnight, hung, robbed and flogged. This was not alone confined to black men, but white men also suffered. The cruelties inflicted upon both during this "reign of terror" are almost indescribable.

This, together with the unjust treatment by the planters in relation to paying wages, renting land, etc., forms the cause of the exodus. We read accounts of where hundreds are leaving their native soil and beginning life anew in another clime. Whether they will be able to withstand the rigorous winters of the West remains to be seen. Already many have perished from exhaustion and cold, not being sufficiently clad, and being wholly without means to procure articles necessary to their comfort. Yet when we look back and see the wrongs heaped upon a poor, downtrodden race we can not but cry: "On with the Exodus!"'"

I had read of hundreds of freedmen leaving their homes and starting for the West, but I never expected to be an eye witness of such a scene. In December, 1879, while visiting Washington, preparatory to going further South, there arrived at the depot from two to three hundred freed people, among which were a number of children. It seems their money gave out as they reached Washington, and here they must remain until means could be obtained to send them further on. Here they were strangers; no where to go, near the edge of evening, yet no where to lay their heads. At this crisis the Rev. Mr. Draper hearing of their situation kindly offered them his church, (St. Paul, 8th St., South Washington), till other arrangements could be made. Here they were made as comfortable as possible, and seemed pleased that they were under shelter. I was told that quite a number had gone on some weeks before, and that they were mostly men. This last party had a majority of women, many of them going on to meet their husbands. The people of Washington were very kind to the strangers, giving them food and clothing in abundance. On the Sunday following their arrival, the pavements were blockaded for squares, all anxious to get a peep at them. The church was not a large one, so to prevent confusion, visitors were requested to pass in one door and out of the other.

Within, a novel sight presented itself; the gallery in the rear of the church had the appearance of a nursery. Children, from a two months' babe upwards, were lying here and there upon the benches, or under them fast asleep. Others were busily engaged in satisfying the inner man. The day I was present there was a reporter gathering scraps of information for his paper. It was really interesting to hear some of them converse. Many appeared to be quite intelligent; says one: "Do you suppose I'd leave my little home, which I owned, and go to a place I know nothing of unless I was compelled to. 'Taint natur. We heard dey killed a man the day we left, dey was so mad, and in some places dey tore up de track to keep us from leaving." Says the reporter: "Suppose you get to Indiana and you find no work there?" Answered: "Den I keeps going till I finds it." They all seemed willing to work if they could only find it to do.

Visitors, as they passed around, on coming to the altar found two small baskets into which they could drop as much money as they felt disposed. This was to assist in defraying the expenses the rest of the journey. As often as a certain amount was made up, they would send away so many at a time.

There was among the company a white woman, whom at first I took to be a leader, as she seemed so energetic, going out and begging proper clothing for the most destitute, distributing food, among them, etc. But upon conversing with her I found I was mistaken. She assured me she was as much a part of the "Exodus," as the rest. That she received no better treatment at her home than the rest did, and she was glad to get away. Some of the prominent lady members of St. Paul's Chapel were most kind in their attentions to the wanderers, leaving their own duties at home to spend days in administering to their comfort; and often were the expressions, "God bless you, de Lord will pay you back, honey," heard on all sides. I did not have an opportunity to see them but once, for when I went again I found they had gone; and it is hoped they have all found good, comfortable homes, in that land towards which their hearts had turned with so much faith and hope.

Terrible Suffering of the Freedmen at Washington

A host of miserable women with children, besides old, crippled and sick persons were driven out of Maryland and sought refuge here. Those who were able to work went out by the day to earn money with which to pay a rent of from five to six dollars for some old shanty, garret, cellar or stable. Hundreds of old persons and children were without shoes and stockings, and were badly frost-bitten. Infants, only a few days old, without a garment, perished with cold. Very few of the older persons had any under-garments, for they came from Maryland and Virginia clothed in rags; very few had comfortable beds and household utensils. The children died off rapidly. During the hot weather the quartermaster's department furnished about eighty coffins per week, mostly for children. "In slavery," the mothers say, "our children never dies; it 'pears like they all dies here." One family lost five out of ten children; another, three out of seven. Sleeping on the shanty and stable floors during the winter brought on colds and pulmonary diseases which terminated the lives of hundreds. The ladies of the district were indefatigable in their efforts to relieve them. Those in Springfield, Mass., kindly solicited aid for these distressed people, gathering clothing of every kind, and were quite successful in sending something to their afflicted brethren.

Educating the Freedmen

This is a matter which absorbed the minds of the North: whether the negro would learn, and eagerly improve the facilities opened to him through his liberation. Almost immediately after the close of the war barracks used by the soldiers were turned into schoolhouses, and it was no rare sight to see a number of these freedmen crowded into them, over whom presided some noble-hearted lady engaged in her duties as school-marm. Would they learn? Let the record of the last fourteen or fifteen years testify.

I can not let this opportunity pass without paying a tribute of respect to the memory of Miss Stebbins, who died while devoting her life to this cause. When I last saw her she was in Washington D.C., at the barracks on the corner of Seventh and O Streets. She lived in one portion of the building, and, although school hours were over, she was instructing two bright, interesting girls in the mysteries of the alphabet. In one corner of the room were boxes of clothing which she distributed among the most needy of her pupils, that they might look presentable day after day. Not only children, but adults attended school, and it was not unusual to see a father and son, a mother and daughter in the same class, eager and anxious to learn. Says one teacher, who kept a night school for the benefit of those who were not able, on account of their work, to attend during the day: "I had a boy present himself as wishing to become a member of the school. After examining him, I found he was pretty well up in all the first principles of arithmetic, except long division; of this he knew nothing. I was astonished to find, after going over a few examples, explaining carefully as I went along, that when the pencil was put in his hand he worked as well as I could." From that night he had no more trouble with long division. That boy was afterwards a hard student at Howard University, and learned to read Latin with ease.

What nation, after years of servitude, has made such rapid strides of improvement? All over the South we find schools with efficient teachers, many of whom were formerly pupils, now going over the same ground others had taken them. The barracks have given way to school buildings of the most modern design. The schools are all graded, the scholars advancing step by step till they reach the topmost round. Perhaps no better examples can be furnished than the District of Columbia, where the school system is fixed upon a firmer and better basis than elsewhere.

The Beginning of the End

The emigration of my people from the Southern States has engaged my attention for some time. In Heathsville, Va., the place of my birth, the colored people are not treated with such severity as in the States further South, for in Heathsville, they have more privileges than they have in Western Virginia. I think the cause of this great emigration is owing to the fact of ill treatment, equal almost to slavery; because of cruelties heaped upon them in the South, and because of the hopelessness of obtaining an education for their children. It was the burden of their complaint; their political rights had been denied them, and every possible advantage had been taken from them, and feeling aggrieved they had looked around for relief, and the only solace offered was to emigrate. In some parts of the South our people labor without hardly wages enough to get them food, which places many of them in a starving condition, and without sufficient clothing. Twenty-five cents a day is considered great wages, taking part corn for pay. My heart has been drawn out for them in sympathy, knowing myself what it was to want, even in Virginia, a meal of victuals.

The emigrants adopted a plan of action to appeal to President Hayes, for him to enforce the laws to protect their rights. Then they appealed to Congress to set apart a territory, or aid them to emigrate to Liberia. Our people lost all hope of bettering their condition at that time. In 1877 they petitioned Congress and President Hayes. Not hearing from this petition, the colored emigrants became exasperated, saying, "let us go any where in God's world to get away from these men who once enslaved us." Many of the white republicans of the South are treated not much better than the colored people, because they are republicans. Since they have emigrated many children, fathers and mothers have died from starvation and exposure, for they were without shelter and nothing to wear, lying on the cold ground, exposed to the winter blasts with only the sky for a covering.

The number of those who poured in upon the State of Kansas, early in the spring of 1879, is known to have been four or five thousand. Steadily has been the flow of the small stream which attracted so little attention, and by the opening of the spring of 1880 over ten thousand arrived, and probably since the spring of 1880 twice the number have emigrated. I think that something must be the cause for their great emigration more than common, for my people are a home-like people; they would never leave the Southern soil if properly treated, or had wages enough to make them comfortable; as a general thing they are home-loving and law abiding citizens. While living South they felt they had "no rights that the white man was bound to respect."

All praise is due to Mrs. Comstock, for her self-denying philanthropy exhibited towards my people, for they must have suffered more had it not been for her endeavors, in writing all over the United States to our most prominent citizens for help to relieve their sufferings. The people in many places have responded to her call. Here, in Norwich, the ladies have come up to the work as they always do where assistance is needed among my people. God bless them for what they have done; hoping they will think of them in the future, as they are still leaving their land of slavery, as they expect the freedom which they have fought for and hoped for. In their going away their places can not be filled, for they were the bone and sinew of the South.

While I write, there are fifty thousand pounds of clothing, sent on in 1879 from England, held at the New York Custom House for duty to be paid on them. They were sent for my people in Kansas. It is wicked to deprive these poor, suffering people of comfortable clothing while so many are dying for the want of it. I trust that the hearts of the people everywhere will be so softened towards my injured people that they will be induced to send them on, even if obliged to pay the duty on them, and not wait for Congress to decide. Shall this people die, who have stood by us in sunshine and storm? Shall we let them suffer for the want of bread, for the want of corn, for the want of clothing? God forbid it! As they stood by the flag once, they stand by it still, because it bespeaks freedom to them and their posterity.

When the Rebel army was five miles from the Capital, and the skirmishers were three miles from Georgetown, when it was conjectured that the assault would take place the next morning, it was then our colored soldiers met the waves of conflict; it was then the bone and sinews of the South saved the Capital of the United States. Aye; my soul listens already to the glad prelude of the song of triumph, welling up from myriads of hearts, and swelling into a paean that fills the vast concave of heaven itself with the deep-toned melodies of an universal jubilee: "Washington is saved!" Then our colored soldiers came up to its rescue, which contradicts the saying, that colored men will not fight. Well did they do their duty, and proved their manhood at Fort Wagner, Fort Moultrie, Petersburg, Milliken's Bend, Fort Fisher, and other places, while their families were left starving at home. We all know that these things are so, although they are not recorded in history with other events of the war.

We hope the time will come when our children, attending white seminaries of learning, may receive medals the same as white students. In Connecticut, and elsewhere, prizes and medals have been and are withheld from our most brilliant scholars of color. In one of our Eastern colleges a colored student was robbed of his essay, and had recourse to a law-suit to have justice done him; but was obliged to write another, and received the prize at his graduation, after the lawsuit was ended. He was obliged to go another year in order to accomplish it. The wrongs of this system will go up before the Throne of Infinite Justice.

The United States ought to be strong enough in intellect, in moral sensibility and Christian feeling, to conquer her prejudices. Until she does, the poet's tribute to "Columbia" as "the land of the free and home of the brave," will be a satire that shall provoke a reproachful smile—attesting her fidelity to justice and liberty, God and man.

The leading question of to-day is, why do the colored people emigrate? Almost every day and week during the spring of 1880, it was discussed among the senators and representatives in Congress, the argument having taken up most of the time; the question also created quite a discussion in 1879; the Southern senators, who were the majority in the Senate, were loath to drop the question.

In conclusion, I must say that the more I contemplate the condition of my people, the more I am convinced that this is only the beginning of the end; but the end is not yet.

FINIS

CLASSICS *in* BLACK STUDIES SERIES